CW00434312

# NAMED TRAINS on L N E R  LINES

by

W.B.YEADON

## Part I:
# The Scottish Trains & The Pullman Trains.

# Acknowledgements

### by the late W.B.Yeadon

To the late Cecil J. Allen, whose 1946 book on titled trains gave me the idea of how fascinating it would be to research and then write a greatly improved and expanded version just dealing with those of the LNER and its successor.

To the officials of the late London and North Eastern Railway whose vibrant ideas on the naming of trains paid off so well in getting not only enthusiasts, but also the public interested in, and travelling by them.

To the names of so many railway photographers who provided such a wealth of visual evidence on which I could base my writing; especially those who were of like mind in regarding the LNER as the line that really mattered.

To Phil Atkins and John Edgington in the Library of the National Railway Museum at York for invaluable help, particularly in producing timetables of the 1920's for me to consult, and for dealing so patiently with my persistent queries. What a joy it has been to have such enthusiastic help.

To my wife and daughter for the encouragement, acceptance and understanding of what has taken up so much of my thoughts for a period now approaching sixty years.

### Publishers Note:

*Although some of the text and a small amount of the photographic material contained in this book have previously been presented in article form elsewhere, this is the first time that all the intended material has been brought together in one cover as was the original intention of the author.*

*We have been able to publish the original manuscript through the courtesy of the Archives at the University of Hull who are now the keeper's of the W.B.Yeadon Railway Archive. In this respect we wish to thank the Archivist and her staff for their usual cheerful and positive demeanor.*

*The catalogue reference relating to the material used in this album is as follows: DYE/1/119, DYE/1/120.*

***First published in the United Kingdom by Book Law Publications***
***382 Carlton Hill, Nottingham, NG4 1JA.***
***Printed and bound by The Amadeus Press, Cleckheaton, West Yorkshire.***

# Named Trains on LNER Lines (On the Drier Side)

## Preface

When travelling by train was the customary way of moving about the country for the general public, most were interested in the train itself, but many found it was obligatory "to go and see which engine we have". In the 1920's the power of advertising was becoming recognised and 'Public Relations' began to be seen to have real advantages. No better item can be cited than that of the "Flying Scotsman" train. Those who were able to use it were proud of doing so, and of saying so. Thus its name was known world-wide despite those who operated it giving no official acceptance to it until 1924. Then they decided there was merit in going along with popular opinion, and naming of LNER trains then flourished.

"Named Trains" needs no explanation. "On the Drier Side" was conjured up by the LNER's Advertising Department to boost their geographical advantage of serving all the holiday resorts on the east coast of Britain, from Lossiemouth on the Moray Firth to Southend on the Thames estuary, and whose rain fall averaged about 40% less than on the west coast of the country.

The chosen train names divide into three categories, the majority indicating the area served. Three were linked with events dear to the whole nation, and these were only used for trains of special importance, of which *THE SILVER JUBILEE* (1935), *CORONATION* (1937), and *THE ELIZABETHAN* (1953) – the British Railways successor to the non-stop *FLYING SCOTSMAN* – were those chosen after they had secured Royal approval. Two others honoured particular people, widely separated in place and time. *THE MASTER CUTLER*, introduced on Monday 6th October 1947, acknowledged the importance of Sheffield's traffic to the LNER, but did not tie itself to any particular person, because the holder of that 350-year old office changed annually, although the LNER Chairman had been the Master Cutler of 1922. The other was quite specific. In November 1927 the LNER announced that from Tuesday 1st May 1928, the 11.20 a.m. Pullman from King's Cross would be extended from Edinburgh to Glasgow, would have two new trains of all-steel cars and would be named *QUEEN OF SCOTS*. What that enigmatic character had to do with the LNER is unknown, but the name provided one of the happiest and most popular choices.

That was the extent for which the LNER was responsible, but there were namings by British Railways from 1948 to 1959 for trains which ran on what had been their lines.

Fourteen of their names indicated the area of operation, and three were connected with the Waverley novels of Sir Walter Scott, these being *THE HEART OF MIDLOTHIAN* (1951), *THE TALISMAN* (1956) and *THE FAIR MAID* (1957), all of them serving Edinburgh - London.

Finally, there was *THE ANGLO-SCOTTISH CAR CARRIER* (1959) which, in the age of the motor car's predominance, provided a more relaxed and congenial journey for passengers travelling long distances. In this volume are the trains named by the LNER in its 25 years existence - 1923 to 1947.

*HATCHETT'S NEW WHITE HORSE CELLAR,*

PICCADILLY

*And WHITE HORSE INN, Fetter Lane, London.*

---

## THE HIGHFLYER COACH,

Every Morning at 6 o'Clock, to

YORK, HULL, LEEDS, NEWCASTLE, EDINBURGH,

AND MOST PARTS OF
*The North of England and Scotland,*

PASSES THROUGH

*Biggleswade, Buckdon, Stilton, Stamford, Grantham, Newark,
Doncaster, Ferrybridge, Thirsk, Northallerton, Darlington,
Durham, Alnwick, &c. &c.*

The utmost Care and Attention paid to Passengers and their Luggage travelling by this Coach, and all Parcels sent by it charged on the most reasonable Terms.

Passengers may stop and Sleep on the Road, and have their Places secured the next Day, without any additional Expence.

N.B. Royal Mail and Telegraph Coaches set out daily from the above Inns to *Manchester, Norwich, Newmarket, Ipswich, Yarmouth, Cambridge, Oxford, Lynn, Leicester, Derby, Northampton, Deal, Dover, Margate, Ramsgate, Worthing, Brighton, Portsmouth, Gosport, Canterbury, Rochester,* and most of the Cities, Manufacturing Towns, and Fashionable Watering Places in the United Kingdom.

Performed by JOHN EAMES & Co.

who cannot hold themselves accountable for Passengers Luggage, or any Package whatever, above the Value of *Five Pounds*, unless the same be specified as such, and an Insurance paid, over and above the common Carriage, at the Time of Delivery at their Offices in Town or to their Agents in the Country.

**The preffered method of travel to the north in 1814. A typical journey from London to Edinburgh undertaken that year left the capital on Thursday 2nd June, stopping one night at Newcastle on Sunday the 5th and continuing on to Edinburgh the next morning. The date of arrival is unknown but the cost was £8 and 8 shilling!**

# Contents

New in April 1922, No.1470 of 4-6-2 Pacific type here in King's Cross station is about to leave with what was possibly the 10 o'clock train for Scotland. This was not a regular rostering because No.1470 was shedded at Doncaster and was only on temporary loan to King's Cross shed. Correspondents and observers of the period state that the second GNR Pacific No.1471 did the honours with the first Pacific hauled 10 o'clock on Saturday 5th August 1922, and that this particular view of No.1470 shows it probably about to depart King's Cross with the 1.40 p.m. to Harrogate on the 28th June 1922.

# INTRODUCTION

## THE POSITION AT THE START OF THE LONDON & NORTH EASTERN RAILWAY

On 1st January 1923, when that railway came into existence, no component of it was then running a single train which had an official title. True, the public had for many years, used the name "Flying Scotchman" for that which, for the previous sixty years, had left King's Cross for Edinburgh at 10 o'clock each weekday, but neither the timetable, nor anything on the train itself, supported the use of that name in any way. To the Great Northern Railway (who set it off from London) it was simply the 'Special Scotch Express', and to their staff it was just "the 10 o'clock". From York, where the North Eastern Railway took it over, that line had no tradition for naming trains, or even engines for that matter. So the two main constituent companies of the LNER contributed nothing on which useful publicity could be based.

The Great Central component named engines extensively, but not trains, and the Great Eastern had entirely discarded the useful start it had made with the pre-war *NORFOLK COAST EXPRESS*. Of the two Scottish components, the Great North of Scotland had no named train. The North British Railway, however, provided not only the LNER's Chairman, William Whitelaw, but had also planted the seeds for train naming. In the 1911 summer they inaugurated their *FIFE COAST EXPRESS* which enabled Glasgow businessmen to do a good day's work in that city combined with joining their families on holiday each evening at resorts between Leven and Crail. A year later, similar facilities were provided for Dunbar, North Berwick and Gullane. That train was the *LOTHIAN COAST EXPRESS*, and whilst both trains were halted by the war, they resumed for the 1921 summer. Their engines carried a headboard showing train name and which led to its later adoption by the LNER. So, for its first five months, the LNER did not have a train in operation, until the two Scottish ones resumed for the 1923 summer.

7th June 1950 was the first Wednesday of the Summer timetable. THE NORSEMAN departed King's Cross on Wednesday and Saturday at 9.15 a.m. The usual load was 350 tons and 188 minutes were allowed for the run to York.

# NAMED TRAINS PRIOR TO 1923

There were very few named trains for the LNER to take over, and only on the North British Railway was the approach of one heralded by a descriptive headboard on the front of the engine. Although known far and wide as "The Flying Scotsman", or often as "Flying Scotchman", this already famous train began its LNER days no more titled than 'Special Scotch Express' in the timetables. Nor did the very mixed coaches forming the 10 o'clock from King's Cross and the 10 o'clock from Edinburgh (Waverley) carry that indication by roof boards. The Great Northern contribution was thus practically nil, as it was also from the North Eastern, from the Great Central and from the Great North of Scotland constituent companies.

The Great Eastern component did have a little to contribute, not a lot, but certainly worthy of mention. From 1st July 1897 they ran their *CROMER EXPRESS* non-stop over the 130 miles from Liverpool Street to North Walsham. In the summer of 1907 they built matching coaches to provide two corridor restaurant car trains for this daily holiday express. In the down direction the train divided at North Walsham, the leading eight coaches (three being restaurant cars) going to Cromer; the next two went direct to Sheringham, and the rear two to Mundesley-on-Sea.

These new train sets were officially titled *NORFOLK COAST EXPRESS* and carried roof boards proclaiming it. Although widely publicised, the locomotive carried no indication that it had charge of the company's most prestigious train.

The 1914-1918 war put an end to this pair of trains and although there was a post-war successor, that train only ran on Mondays, Fridays and Saturdays and to a much less exacting schedule. The title was not revived, and so there was no more than tradition for the LNER to inherit from its Great Eastern constituent.

The remaining company, the North British Railway, had a couple of summer holiday trains, and many years usage of indicating the destination of trains on their engine. From the early 1900's it was a widespread custom for Edinburgh and Glasgow area families to take a house by the sea for the school holidays which meant most of July and August. Their bread-winner could only be wholly with them for up to two weeks, but as many resorts on the east coast were within thirty miles of Edinburgh and eighty-five miles of Glasgow, a series of reasonably priced weekly tickets, and a fast, attractive train service could persuade business and professional men to travel daily so as to have the evenings and weekends sharing in the holiday pleasures of their families.

To get the benefit of this traffic potential, the NBR put on the *FIFE COAST EXPRESS* for the summer of 1910, but running from Glasgow only on Fridays to resorts from Leven to Crail, and returning from them to Glasgow only on Monday mornings. In 1911 the service was daily, leaving Glasgow at 4.20 p.m. and non-stop over the 66$\frac{1}{2}$ miles to Leven, then calling at the other seven resorts before termination at Crail. 'Scott' Class engines were used, and they carried a headboard showing the train name.

For the summer of 1912, resorts on the south side of the Firth of Forth were catered for in a similar way, but with an eight coach train, as against the four coaches normally on the Fife trains, and it carried *LOTHIAN COAST EXPRESS* as a headboard. This train began on Monday 3rd June 1912 at 7.55 a.m. when a two-coach set left Dunbar, and at Drem picked up three coaches and a restaurant car which had left North Berwick at 8.00 a.m. at that same time the other two-coach set left Gullane, its coupling-up at Longniddry completing the train. A 'Scott' Class 4-4-0 had it into Waverley at 8.43 a.m. and into Glasgow (Queen St.) at 9.49 a.m. after making the first of what became regular sixty-minute runs between those two stations.

Return from Glasgow was at 3.50 p.m., from Waverley at 4.56 p.m. giving arrival at Gullane at 5.34 p.m.; North Berwick at 5.40 p.m. and Dunbar at 5.45 p.m.. Current working hours meant that most of the passengers would be those with employment in Edinburgh, but the inter-city timings facilitated a day's business in Glasgow for Edinburgh's professional people as well as for shopping. The return train also provided relief to the through Glasgow-Leeds express leaving at 4.00 p.m. This latter train, which began in July 1901, was a most well-used and popular train but which, due to North Eastern Railway apathy on train naming, had to run for almost fifty years before getting a name.

Having just established themselves, the Fife Coast and the Lothian Coast trains became casualties of the 1914-1918 war, but they were resumed for the 1921 summer and when the London & North Eastern Railway was formed it lost no time at trying to regain this traffic. On Friday 1st June 1923, the *LOTHIAN COAST EXPRESS* began that season with a set of coaches newly painted into standard L&NER livery.

**The Scottish Trains:**

| | |
|---|---|
| FLYING SCOTSMAN | (1/10/24). |
| ABERDONIAN | (11/7/27). |
| HIGHLANDMAN | (11/7/27). |
| NIGHT SCOTSMAN | (11/7/27). |

**The Pullman Trains:**

| | |
|---|---|
| HARROGATE PULLMAN | (9/7/23). |
| HARROGATE-EDINBURGH PULLMAN | (Began 13/7/25; named 11/7/27). |
| QUEEN OF SCOTS | (1/5/28). |
| SHEFFIELD PULLMAN | (2/6/24 to 30/5/25). |
| MANCHESTER PULLMAN | (1/6/25 to 19/9/25). |
| WEST RIDING PULLMAN | (Began 21/9/25; named 1/1/27 to 28/9/35). |
| YORKSHIRE PULLMAN | (30/9/35). |
| WEEKEND PULLMAN | (16/7/27 to 25/9/27). |
| HARROGATE SUNDAY PULLMAN | (6/5/28). |
| CLACTON PULLMAN | (1923 to 1927 Summers). |
| CLACTON SUNDAY PULLMAN | (6/5/28 to 23/9/28). |
| EASTERN BELLE | (1929 to 1939 Summers). |

The above listed trains dealt with in this particular volume. The dates appertain to the start and finish of the services or as otherwise indicated.

A splendid view of Haymarket's A4 No.4483 departing platform 8 at Newcastle on its journey north with the *FLYING SCOTSMAN* in June 1938. The 'non-stop' season in 1938 did not start for this train until 4th July.

When the LNER took them over, the 10 o'clock expresses from London and from Edinburgh were normally hauled by 4-4-2 type engines with changes at Grantham, York and Newcastle. No.1460 shedded at King's Cross is coasting down the 1 in 200 approaching New Barnet with the 10.00 a.m. from Edinburgh which also had through coaches from Aberdeen and Glasgow. This Atlantic had taken over at Grantham.

# FLYING SCOTSMAN (1924-1950)
# THE FLYING SCOTSMAN (From 1950)

The "Flying Scotsman" name is known world-wide, but to some it is the engine of that ilk and not the train. The LNER named both in 1924, the engine in February, for participation in the British Empire Exhibition at Wembley, and the train in September when two new eleven-coach sets went into service on it. The general public seem to have called the train the Flying Scotchman from at least the 1880's, but through to their demise at the end of 1922, none of the three East Coast railways on which it ran, ever regarded it as having any official claim to the name.

At Grouping, the LNER set up an Advertising Department, with W.M.Teasdale in charge of it. Brought up on the North Eastern Railway, he had no tradition for train naming, but probably four factors gelled and resulted in the name gaining official recognition. The Chairman came from a railway which did name trains; the July 1923 naming of the *HARROGATE PULLMAN* had proved attractive - successful; his job was to make the LNER known to a wider public, who did not need persuading that *FLYING SCOTSMAN* was a train of prestige; and he had new train sets to show off. These had triplet articulated dining cars, with a kitchen using electricity instead of gas for cooking which gave him the chance to invite the Press to inspect one of the new sets, and give them hospitality on a trip to York and back to London. All their reports would call the train the *FLYING SCOTSMAN* and so it became - officially.

For more than another seven years the "Flying" was a distinct misnomer, for the train was limited to taking at least $8^1/_4$ hours for the London-Edinburgh journey, an average of no more than 47.6 miles per hour, when around 60 m.p.h. was the accepted norm for a top express. At that speed the $8^1/_4$ hours could have been cut to $6^1/_2$ hours which the Gresley Pacifics could have achieved. The $8^1/_4$ hours minimum stemmed from an agreement made in 1895 by the East and West Coast Main Lines that they would not cut below it for trains between London and Edinburgh and Glasgow. When that agreement was made, the "10 o'clock" was still leaving King's Cross behind an engine with only single driving wheels, whether of the 4-2-2 or 2-2-2 type, but with a load vastly different from what it had become when the LNER took it over.

In 1922 it usually left London with two engines, a GNR Atlantic piloted by a 4-4-0 tender engine (or even an 0-6-2 tank) at least until the climb to Potters Bar had been surmounted. The Atlantic changed to another of the same class at Grantham which took it through to York. There, the North Eastern Railway put on one of their Atlantics, either of their two, or three-cylinder type, which at Newcastle, was similarly replaced to run through to Edinburgh. The Up train, which also left at 10 o'clock from Edinburgh, had corresponding haulage arrangements.

At Grouping, the GNR and the NER both had two new 4-6-2 type engines to contribute, which eliminated piloting, and when, during 1923 and 1924, the Gresley design multiplied, engine changing could be reduced to only at Grantham and at Newcastle. The new train sets of 1924, although loading to around 400 tons, were well within their scope, especially at speeds averaging under 50 m.p.h. One of the sets was sent to Scottish Area, and on 19th September 1924 was taken by ex-NBR Atlantic No.9878 from Edinburgh through to Aberdeen. It returned behind No.9872, which worked through

from Aberdeen. The eleven bogie coaches included a three-coach dining set (1st class saloon, kitchen, 3rd class saloon), but the bogie brake van at each end carried a 'Rebuilt 1924' plate, and retained their old numbers, e.g. 219J which indicated East Coast Joint Stock. With the limitation on speed, other aspects for boosting the train's image had to be considered.

Experience in running the Gresley Pacifics (LNER Class A1) showed that small, inexpensive modifications could reduce their coal consumption considerably, and in the 1927 summer, we saw in which direction progress was to be made. On July 11th a relief train to *FLYING SCOTSMAN* left King's Cross at 9.50 a.m. behind No.4475 FLYING FOX and initiated non-stop running to Newcastle, which at 268 miles was then the world's longest. The West Coast countered later that year by running their *ROYAL SCOT* London to Glasgow train non-stop to, and from, Carlisle which increased the record to 299 miles. The LNER reply was quick, innovative and effective.

On 1st May 1928, two new train sets each left at 10 o'clock from King's Cross and Edinburgh and ran non-stop over the 392.8 miles to the other capital city. Nor was that any specially prepared 'one-off' effort. Each summer in the twelve years to 1939, every Monday to Saturday saw successful operation of the pair of *FLYING SCOTSMAN* non-stop trains. All GN 4-6-2 engines had a tender carrying 8 tons of coal and 5000 gallons of water and use of the latter could be replenished from the six sets of track troughs traversed en route. But for more than eight hours, no fireman could be required to keep $41^1/_4$ square feet of grate adequately coaled. Two firemen were thus essential, each coping with half the run,

The second Great Northern Railway 4-6-2 No.1471, new in July 1922, was also allocated to Doncaster shed for its normal work. Early in September 1922 it was loaned to King's Cross for special load testing and here at Hornsey, they have used it for the 10.00 a.m. Edinburgh express before returning it to Doncaster.

*(right)* The 10 o'clock from Edinburgh was hauled to Newcastle by a North Eastern Railway 4-4-2 shedded at Gateshead, both 2-cylinder Class V (as here) and 3-cylinder Class Z being used. A similar engine was used between Newcastle and York.

*(below)* South of York, Great Northern engines worked the trains, Grantham shed providing the power to and from York. Atlantic No.281's only shed was Grantham and here it is leaving York on a 10 o'clock from Edinburgh to King's Cross.

In the LNER's first year the 4-4-2 engines continued to be used and out of King's Cross terminus, heavy trains were given a pilot engine for the climb to Potter's Bar. D2 Class No.1336 of Hitchin shed assists C1 No.1406 of Grantham with the 10 o'clock from King's Cross.

*(opposite, top)* Between February and September 1923, ten new Pacific's went into traffic, and a start could then be made on saving a change of engine. In the 1924 summer, a King's Cross A1 took the Down train through to York from where a Grantham A1 took the Up train through to London.

*(opposite, bottom)* Two new eleven-coach sets were built in 1924 - for the 10 o'clock trains - and on 29th September one set was used for this press run to York from King's Cross. In the resultant publicity all the papers referred to the train as "Flying Scotsman" and, at long last, that name was adopted and became used officially. A1 No.1471 was Doncaster shedded and took no part in the regular working of the 10 o'clock trains.

THE FLYING SCOTSMAN.

Gateshead shed still worked the trains between Edinburgh and York with a change of engine during the call at Newcastle (Central). This is the Up train on the Royal Border Bridge over the river Tweed with the summer load of thirteen coaches.

Gateshead's C7 Class No.706 carried this first style of company initials from 30th May 1923 to 25th November 1924 and here at Aycliffe is taking the Down train from York to Newcastle.

*(left)* The North Eastern Railway managed to build two 4-6-2 engines very late in 1922 and they were allocated to Gateshead shed who used them mainly between Newcastle and Edinburgh, including some work on the 10 o'clock trains which No.2400 is doing here.

*(opposite)* In September and October 1924, Gateshead received ten new Gresley 4-6-2's built by the N.B. Locomotive Co. and until 1928 these were their preference for working the *FLYING SCOTSMAN* trains on the Newcastle-Edinburgh legs of the journey as No.2572 is performing in this view.

*continued from page 7./* and it was unreasonable for their inactive four hours to be spent on a noisy, hot and swaying footplate; the driver's concentration had to be considered, also, whilst there was adequate space, it was clearly undesirable for four men to remain on the footplate throughout.

Gresley solved that problem by designing a tender with the same coal and water capacities, but including a passage eighteen inches wide by five feet high through the eighteen feet long tender, with a vestibule connection to the first coach of the train. So, both crews could have comparative rest, either before or after their work on the engine. The service needed a minimum of four corridor type tenders, one each on the actual runs and one each at the London and Edinburgh sheds on a stand-by engine to ensure availability for punctual departure every weekday at both ends. The corridor type tender was interchangeable with the normal type, but having to make a change in a hurry was to be avoided. Ten of the corridor tenders were built, so first thoughts had obviously been that a pair of trains other than the

*FLYING SCOTSMAN* were under consideration. It is understood that one of the night sleeping car expresses running non-stop was contemplated, but that was never put into effect.

The Up train on 1st May 1928 also brought another innovation, from Scottish Area to the Southern Area. From 1924 the train name had only appeared on coach roof boards, but on the NBR it had been customary to draw attention to their notable trains by equipping the engine with a headboard. So Haymarket shed deemed it proper for the engine of the first Up train to carry one showing *FLYING SCOTSMAN* in black on a white background Previously their boards had been dark red with white lettering. King's Cross shed had been upstaged by this publicity gimmick, and thought it prudent to follow suit, but it was Tuesday 15th May before one of their engines left London so adorned, No.4476 ROYAL LANCER being their first to carry one. This London board could be identified as "Flying" was closer spaced than on the Scottish board. Enthusiasts will be interested to know in detail, which engines were used on the non-stops.

**1928 Season** - *1st May to 23rd September:*

For the first non-stop out of King's Cross, pride of place was appropriately accorded to A1 Class No.4472, the engine with a FLYING SCOTSMAN nameplate over each middle coupled wheel. It returned the following day on the Up train, but the next return trip was done by No.2546, which did not

become a regular performer. No.4472 took up the running again, and by the end of May, it had done seven double journeys. It was then used steadily throughout the summer, along with Nos.4476 and 2547 (which had acquired corridor tender from No.2546) as the regular choices. No.2552 did two return trips in June, and after No.4475 had completed a general repair, it was used from 19th August, with the corridor tender from No.2552.

From the Edinburgh end, A3 Class No.2580 made the first five trips, and then regular trips before A3 No.2573 was used. Both these engines (along with No.2569, which was never used) were on loan from Gateshead shed, because the Pacifics allocated to Haymarket shed were only in the process of changing to the longer travel valve gear necessary for reduced coal consumption. However, Haymarket's No.2563 took the corridor tender from No.2569 and first went south with the non-stop on 25th May, alternating then with No.2580 for the remainder of the 1928 running.

On 2nd July, Haymarket's No.2564 exchanged tenders with No.2573, and became reserve engine at the Scottish end, but remained so during that year's operation.

**1929 Season** - *8th July to 22nd September:*

The opening return trips were taken by Haymarket's No.2566, and No.2547 from King's Cross shed. Then King's Cross used it along with Nos.4472, 4475, and 4476 but also started new A3 No.2750 on a long association with the non-stops.

Work from the Scottish end was done by Nos.2563, 2564, and 2566; the other two Haymarket Pacifics, Nos.2565 and 2567, never participating in the non-stop running. No.2565 did have a corridor type tender coupled to it for a while, but only from the 20th March to 4th July (which was prior to the start of the non-stop running that year) when No.2566 took it over, and No.2567 never had a corridor type tender.

**1930 Season** - *8th July to 21st September:*

A curious feature was that King's Cross shedded engines worked both the inaugural trips, A3 No.2746 taking the Down train and No.4472 bringing the one from Edinburgh having worked there on Sunday 6th July. For the rest of the season, King's Cross continued to use its regulars - A1's Nos.4472, 4475 and 4476 and A3 No.2750 joined by No.2746 with 4472 and 2750 doing most of the work.

The noteworthy workings came from the Scottish end, because except for one trip, three of their engines sufficed for the full season - Nos.2563 and 2796 (first used on 10th July) being regulars but the star performer was No.2795 CALL BOY which had a run of twenty-eight consecutively, twenty-four on weekdays and four on the balancing Sunday working. The exception was a return trip made by the high-pressure compound No.10000, Up on 31st July and back on 1st August which it completed successfully but never repeated.

**1931 Season** - *20th July to 13th September:*

This was the final year when non-stop running had to be spun out to $8^{1}/_{4}$ hours and no more than six regular performers coped with it, Haymarket relying entirely on their two A3's Nos.2795 and 2796. From King's Cross the customary A1's 4472, 4475, 4476 and A3 No.2750 were used.

**1932 Season** - *18th July to 11th September:*

The ending of the East Coast/West Coast agreement enabled the non-stop running time to be cut to $7^{1}/_{2}$ hours, putting the average speed up to 52.3 m.p.h. The 10 o'clock departure times were retained, so arrival became 5.30 p.m. instead of 6.15 p.m. Again, King's Cross used its 'seasoned' performers 4472, 4476, 2547 and 2746 whilst Haymarket needed only Nos.2563 and 2795.

**1933 Season** - *17th July to 10th September:*

The reliability of Haymarket engines continued with No.2796 on the first Up train and along with No.2795, those two were all they needed to use. King's Cross did put some variety in, using two fresh ones, an A3 class No.2744 and A1 No.4474 which acquired a corridor tender from No.2547; but they also sent out Nos.4472, 4475 and 2746.

One of the very rare failures occurred on the last day when No.4472's big end ran hot and it had to come off at Grantham. The replacement was A1 No.2556 which did not have a corridor tender, so both crews had to remain on the footplate through to Edinburgh. The twelve coach train left Grantham nineteen minutes late, was fourteen down at York, only seven down through Newcastle and was into Waverley three minutes *early*, even on the $7^{1}/_{2}$ hour schedule.

**1934 Season** - *9th July to 15th September:*

No.4472 took the first Down train and No.2796 was the first from Edinburgh and the season concluded with No.2744 on the last Up and No.2795 on the last Down workings.

Once more Nos.2795 and 2796 were all that Haymarket needed, and those used by King's Cross were Nos.4474, 4475, 4476 and 2746.

**1935 Season** - *8th July to 14th September:*

No.4472 again had the first Down train and No.2795 the first Up, whilst the season was rounded off by No.2744 on the last Up and (who else?) but No.2795 going home with the final Down train.

Others used from the London end were Nos.4475, 4476 and 2746, 2750. However, Haymarket's Nos.2795 and 2796 had their almost total monopoly broken by another A3, only six months old, and the last of that class to be built. No.2508 BROWN JACK took over No.2563's

corridor tender and made its first Up run on 15th August.

**1936 Season** - *6th July to 12th September:*

Another fifteen minutes were pared from the running time and this was the last year in which the A1 and A3 classes had the limelight. No.4475 took the first Down and also brought in the last Up train, whilst No.2508 opened from Edinburgh, but No.2795 on the last Down working was making its final non-stop appearance.

As customary, No.2796 took some of the Haymarket turns, and King's Cross did not stray outside reliable performers Nos.4472, 4476, 2744, 2746 and 2750, in addition to No.4475. But before the next summer season, the ten 1928-built corridor tenders had all been taken from the A1 and A3 classes.

**1937 Season** - *5th July to 11th September:*

Running time was now cut to seven hours and streamlined A4 class were assigned to the non-stops, having been equipped with the refurbished 1928 corridor tenders. Even so, No.2750 managed to put in a last stand for A3 class. It had lost its corridor tender on 13th November 1936 but on 30th June 1937 acquired one which was spare because the A4 to which it was allocated was not completed until October. So on 6th and 7th August, No.2750 went to Edinburgh and back on the non-stop.

But this year saw the start of the A4 monopoly of London-Edinburgh non-stop workings which, by steam, was never to be broken. No.4484 had the first from London and No.4482 that from Edinburgh and the last ones had No.4492 coming south and No.4485 going north. The brunt from King's Cross was taken by No.4492 assisted by No.4483 and A3 No.2750 on its single return trip. Nos.4484 and 4485 were all that were needed by Haymarket shed.

On 1st July 1925 the centenary of the Stockton & Darlington Railway was celebrated by a procession of engines and trains in which Raven Pacific No.2400 hauled one of the 1924-built eleven-coach sets for the *FLYING SCOTSMAN.*

The first step to eliminate a York stop to change engines was taken on 11th July 1927 when the 9.50 a.m. relief train ran non-stop to Newcastle. On its first day, King's Cross shed's No.4475 is running through York station, on the 268 mile non-stop trip.

There was no non-stop corresponding run from Newcastle to London in relief to the Up *FLYING SCOTSMAN*. No.2578 BAYARDO, here passing Durham, was probably borrowed by Gateshead because its allocated shed was Heaton.

The first non-stop *FLYING SCOTSMAN* leaving King's Cross on the 1st May 1928 with the appropriate motive power.

The two engine crews for the first Up non-stop run at Edinburgh (Waverley) on 1st May 1928.

The first Up non-stop leaving Waverley and carrying the first headboard.

**1938 Season** - *4th July to 10th September:*

Two complete new train sets were introduced and as they had electrically driven atmosphere conditioning in every coach, that added appreciably to the load to be hauled. Only A4 class were used, No.4482 took the first Down, No.4489 the first Up, No.4498 the last Up and No.4487 the final Down trains.

Most unusually, Haymarket used four A4's, Nos.4482, 4487, 4490 and 4491. King's Cross shed only used three, concentrating on the quality of Nos.4489, 4498 and 2512.

**1939 Season** - *3rd July to 2nd September:*

A total of seven engines again covered the operation, five used in the previous year and Nos.4483 and 4484 taking the places of Nos.2512 and 4491. The non-stops were scheduled to have run until 9th September but the outbreak of war caused it to cease and it was then nine years before it was able to resume. Before that was possible, the LNER as such, had ceased to exist.

### Winter Services.

Although the summer non-stop was the glamour train and attracted the attention, it only ran for an average of ten weeks each year. Every weekday morning of the other forty-two weeks one *FLYING SCOTSMAN* left King's Cross and another left Edinburgh Waverley at 10 o'clock as they had been doing almost without any break or alteration of departure time since 1862.

In the 1930's these trains provided one of the hardest locomotive jobs in this country especially after the new 1938 train sets were introduced. The overall time was no more than seven hours and twenty minutes, including calls at Grantham, York, Newcastle (where engines were changed) and Berwick.

Often regarded as just a London-Edinburgh train it included two coaches which went on to Glasgow, one for Perth and three for Aberdeen, making fourteen in place of the twelve on the non-stop. At weekends, particularly to London, it was often strengthened to fifteen or even sixteen coaches which meant something like 600 tons behind the tender which, at the start of each run weighed about 60 tons, also to be hauled.

### "Is Your Journey Really Necessary?"

During the 1939-1945 war the *FLYING SCOTSMAN* was one of only three trains to retain a name (The *ABERDONIAN* and the *NIGHT SCOTSMAN* were the others) but the carrying of headboard and coach roof boards was banned.

On Bank Holiday Saturday 2nd August 1941, I was observing on Doncaster station and first came the 9.50 a.m. from King's Cross running as a relief as far as Newcastle which passed through at 1.10 p.m. with A4 class No.4464 on nineteen coaches and a van. The "Scotsman" itself arrived at 1.35 p.m. with eighteen coaches hauled by No.2582 then still in A1 class. At 1.49 p.m. A3 class No.2505 arrived with fifteen coaches as the Glasgow portion running separately. So the 10 o'clock that day needed fifty-two bogie coaches to carry those whose journey was - or those who considered it was - necessary!

In the other direction, at 3.15 p.m. the Up 10 o'clock from Edinburgh went through with A1 No.2543 on nineteen coaches; at 3.32 p.m. a relief to the 10.10 a.m. from Edinburgh had an A3 class on fifteen coaches and that left at 3.42 p.m. The 10.10 a.m. itself arrived at 3.47 p.m. behind A1 class No.2568 on seventeen coaches and Doncaster station staff got it away again at 3.50 p.m. So, fifty-one coaches had to be provided for those going south who 'needed' to travel.

The circumstances that day were undoubtedly somewhat exceptional, but throughout the war, some eighteen absolutely packed coaches were every *FLYING SCOTSMAN'S* daily load and often there were twenty or more. I doubt if the new C.M.E. could have found much to cavil at re Gresley's 2 to 1 gear that day.

With such loads, and no question of having a pilot, the running time had to be extended to an average of 8³/₄ to 9 hours for the full journey because station calls were many and lengthy. Just recall that when an A4 was used, its design had been based on dealing with a 220 ton train load at 70 m.p.h. not 600 plus tons at around 45 m.p.h. average speed. Whilst the A1 and A3 engines had the names of racehorses, those of Shire dray horses would have been more in keeping with what was expected of them at that time.

*(below)* The original Scottish headboard, first carried on that 1st May 1928 Up journey and with 'Flying' spaced out.

A London engine on Up non-stop still without headboard on the Up train, Saturday 12th May 1928. Note 3rd and 4th vehicles are twelve-wheeled clerestory roof type coaches, unusual inclusions after 1924, but featured in photos pages 9 and 10.

A London engine on the Down non-stop, Friday 25th May 1928, using a headboard made at King's Cross shed with different letter spacing, "Flying" being more compressed.

When the non-stop began, Scottish based Pacifics had not then been changed to long travel valves which were needed to cut the coal consumption. Haymarket's No.2563 was made ready to make its first south bound run on 25th May 1928 and here is about to pass through Newcastle (Central) on a north bound working. It then shared the 1928 runs with No.2580 from the Scottish end.

*(above)* The operation of the non-stops depended on the ability to change crew about the half-way mark and the corridor tender provided this facility. No.4476 was one of the three engines used regularly from the London end in 1928, No.4472 and No.2547 being the others.

*(left)* The non-stops only ran in the summer season, but after 1928 it became usual for the headboard to be carried throughout the year. Gateshead's No.2577 has the normal winter load of twelve coaches on the Down between Newcastle and Edinburgh in 1929.

Engines shedded at King's Cross, Gateshead and Haymarket normally monopolised working of this train, but No.2743 was almost entirely shedded at Doncaster. However, from 15th March to 17th July 1936 it was at Gateshead and here at Potters Bar it has the Down train. Note the headboard has the Gill sans lettering adopted as standard in 1932.

Haymarket's A1 No.2566 was used on the first 1929 non-stop from King's Cross as here on 7th July. Of their five A1's they used No.2563 most often, and Nos.2564 and 2566 occasionally but never Nos.2565 and 2567 on non-stops.

By the 1930 season Haymarket had the A3 class higher pressure engines available and to the end of the 1936 non-stops, used Nos.2795 and 2796 almost exclusively. In 1930 No.2795 made twenty-eight runs consecutively. The reserve engine until 1935 was No.2563.

*(left)* No.2508 was the final A3 to be built and went new to Haymarket in February 1935. Its first non-stop was on 15th August 1935, and with No.2795 it was used frequently in the 1936 season. Here on 8th August 1936 it has the Up train at Mutton Lane bridge, Potters Bar.

*(below)* For the 1937 season the time was cut to seven hours, so all except one trip was worked by the streamlined A4 class. Down on 6th August and back on the 7th, King's Cross used No.2750. Here on the Down train it is passing Sandy.

*(right)* In 1930 Gateshead shed received five new A3's, Nos.2595 to 2599, which they then used regularly for the 168 mile run to and from London when the *FLYING SCOTSMAN* made calls at York and Grantham. On this Up run, early in 1939 at Grantham, note that the headboard is in the position normally used on the streamlined engines.

*(below)* No.2597, here on the Up train, takes water from Langley troughs and has the original headboard provided by the Scottish Area. Although the tender is high sided it does not have a corridor.

*(below, right)* No.2599, here in 1932 or 1933 at Greenwood on the Up train - with a pair of articulated coaches at the front of the normal set - has begun to coast down the 1 in 200 from Potters Bar to King's Cross.

No.10000, the one-off, high pressure 4-cylinder compound engine with water-tube boiler, made just one return trip on the non-stop *FLYING SCOTSMAN* from Edinburgh to London on 31st July 1930 and here is returning from King's Cross on 1st August.

*(right)* When the non-stop operated, it also had a through portion to and from Aberdeen and, in the timetables, the train to which it was attached north of Edinburgh was shown as *THE FLYING SCOTSMAN* but no headboard was carried outside the summer season. The 10 o'clock had portions attached for Aberdeen, Perth and Glasgow but only on the Perth portion was an engine headboard used. The Up working was run by a St Margarets shedded engine as here at Haymarket West Junction.

*(below)* Here, in May 1933, the Perth portion is just leaving that station with St Margaret's D11 No.6398 in charge. Where the upper lamp iron was used for the headboard, this could clearly pose problems on engines with an iron at the top of the smokebox.

*(below right)* Engines shedded at Perth - as was D49 No.250 - also took part in this working. With the headboard entirely above the smokebox, this shows the risk of it being blown off at speed also, possible interference of the smoke clearing from the chimney.

From their introduction in September 1935, A4 class began to take the *FLYING SCOTSMAN* workings. The engine which had gone to Newcastle on the Friday evening *SILVER JUBILEE* returned to its King's Cross shed next day on the Up *FLYING SCOTSMAN*. No.2509 is leaving Darlington on Saturday 18th October 1935. Note the initial use of the upper lamp iron for the headboard.

Saturday 30th January 1937 and the second of the A4 class No.2510 passes Low Fell taking the Up train from Newcastle to London. By then an instruction had been issued for A4's to carry the headboard on the centre lamp iron, at the base of the smokebox, to minimise the danger of blowing off at the higher speeds at which this class worked.

The building of more A4 class from December 1936 and their taking corridor tenders from the A1 and A3 engines resulted in the *FLYING SCOTSMAN* being A4 hauled the year round. All Haymarket worked 'non-stops' were taken by either No.4484 or No.4485. Here No.4484, entering King's Cross station, has come non-stop from Edinburgh in seven hours.

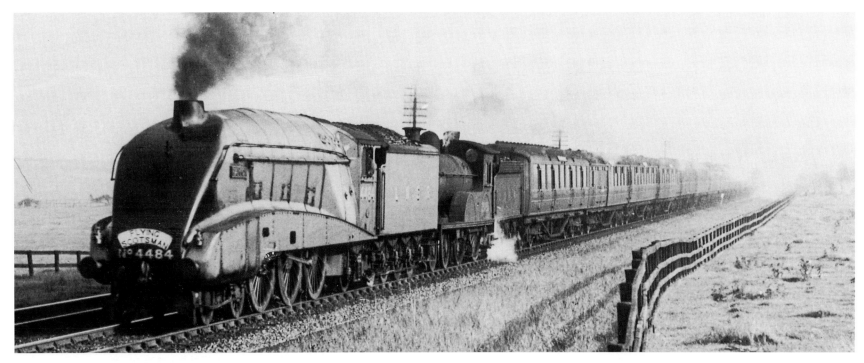

(above) A4 class only had an assisting engine in very exceptional circumstances, and it is a pity this load cannot be determined. The helper is Tweedmouth shedded No.2025 of Class D20. As was customary in the Scottish Area, the assistant was put behind the train engine for the latter's driver to keep responsibility for the running.

(opposite) Until war caused cessation of streamlined high speed trains after 1st September 1939, No.2511 was shedded at Gateshead as the reserve for the SILVER JUBILEE Up train. Then it normally worked to and from Edinburgh so that it was rarely seen on the FLYING SCOTSMAN as in this 1939 visit to London.

(right) C7 class No.2206 helping A4 No.4900 take the Up train from Newcastle to York, could well have been used conveniently to return the C7 to its home shed at York. North Eastern Area put assistant engines in front, but here at Low Fell, the A4 appears to be doing most of the work.

| MILES | STATIONS. Etc. | | SCHED | ACTUAL | SPEEDS |
|---|---|---|---|---|---|
| 0.0 | KING'S CROSS | ... ... | 0 | 0 00 | - |
| 2.5 | Finsbury Park | ... ... | - | 7 33 | 35 |
| 5.0 | Wood Green | ... ... | - | 10 58 | 50 |
| 9.2 | New Barnet | ... ... | - | 16 55 | 40 |
| 12.7 | Potter's Bar | ... ... | - | 22 17 | 39 |
| 17.7 | HATFIELD | ... ... | 24 | 27 22 | 76 |
| 23.5 | Woolmer Green | ... ... | - | 32 17 | 65 |
| 28.6 | Stevenage | ... ... | - | 36 36 | 72 |
| 31.9 | HITCHIN | ... ... | 38 | 39 07 | 85 |
| 37.0 | Arlesley | ... ... | - | 42 33 | 91 |
| 41.1 | Biggleswade | ... ... | - | 45 30 | 82 |
| 44.1 | Sandy | ... ... | - | 47 46 | 74 |
| 47.5 | Tempsford | ... ... | - | 50 28 | 77 |
| 51.7 | St. Neots | ... ... | - | 53 55 | 72 |
| 56.0 | Offord | ... ... | - | 57 13 | 80/67~ |
| 58.9 | HUNTINGDON | ... ... | 59 | 59 48 | 70 |
| 63.4 | Abbot's Ripton | ... ... | - | 64 05 | 59# |
| 69.4 | Holme | ... ... | - | 68 30 | 85 |
| 72.6 | Yaxley | ... ... | - | 71 05 | - |
| 76.4 | PETERBOROUGH | ... ... | 76 | 75 23 | 27* |
| 79.5 | Werrington Junction | ... ... | - | 80 09 | 58 |
| 84.8 | Tallington | ... ... | - | 85 18 | 66 |
| 88.6 | Essendine | ... ... | - | 88 50 | 62 |
| 92.2 | Little Bytham | ... ... | - | 92 17 | 60 |
| 97.1 | Corby | ... ... | - | 97 35 | 53 |
| 100.1 | Stoke Summit Box | ... ... | - | 101 03 | 48 |
| 102.1 | Great Ponton | ... ... | - | 103 03 | 71 |
| 105.5 | GRANTHAM | ... ... | 110 | 107 55 | - |
| 4.2 | Barkstone | ... ... | - | 7 55 | 68 |
| 9.9 | Claypole | ... ... | - | 12 35 | 79 |
| 14.6 | NEWARK | ... ... | 15 | 16 19 | 60« |
| 21.9 | Crow Park | ... ... | - | 23 25 | 70 |
| 28.2 | Markham Summit Box | ... ... | - | 29 27 | 57 |
| 33.1 | RETFORD | ... ... | 33 | 34 00 | 55* |
| 38.4 | Ranskill | ... ... | - | 39 13 | 69 |
| 42.2 | Bawtry | ... ... | - | 42 30 | 66 |
| 44.0 | Mile Post 149° | ... ... | - | 44 14 | 58° |
| 45.8 | Rossington | ... ... | - | 45 58 | 74 |
| 50.5 | DONCASTER | ... ... | 49 | 50 18 | 60* |
| 54.7 | Shaftholme Junction | ... ... | 53 | 54 18 | 67 |
| 60.5 | Balne | ... ... | - | 59 21 | 70 |
| 64.3 | Templehirst | ... ... | - | 62 41 | 72 |
| 66.9 | SELBY | ... ... | 67 | 67 45 | 20 S |
| 73.0 | Riccall | ... ... | - | 73 20 | 61 |
| 78.5 | Naburn | ... ... | - | 78 35 | 66 |
| 80.7 | Chaloner's Whin Junction | ... ... | - | 80 40 | 57* |
| 82.7 | YORK | ... ... | 83 | 84 55 | - |

On this and the following page appears a log, laid out in tabular form, of the remarkable run carried out with A4 No.4490 EMPIRE OF INDIA, on the 26th September 1938 with the Down *FLYING SCOTSMAN*. Alongside the table appears the notes compiled to accompany the log. The performance of the locomotive and its crew speak for themselves.

L.N.E.R. KING'S CROSS-NEWCASTLE.

"FLYING SCOTSMAN"

ENGINE:A4 No.4490 EMPIRE OF INDIA (Haymarket shed).
DRIVER: Dalrymple,
FIREMAN: Armstrong,
(Gateshead shed).
LOAD: 17 coaches.
WEIGHT:593 tons tare, 635 tons gross.

Schedule was improved on to a total of 4 minutes gross and 5 minutes net, notwithstanding a schedule of 57.5 m.p.h. from King's Cross to Grantham and 59.8 m.p.h. from there to York. The 54.9 miles from Hatfield to Yaxley were run in 43 mins 43 secs at an average of 75.3 m.p.h. (including the usual slack over Offord curves, and the three mile ascent at 1 in 200 beyond Huntingdon). The engine displayed its ability to maintain between 72 and 74 m.p.h. with this heavy train over the comparatively level stretch between Sandy and St. Neot's. After the Peterborough slowing, a speed of 66 m.p.h. was attained on the level to Tallington and the final three miles at 1 in 178 up the bank to Stoke were breasted at a lowest rate of 48 m.p.h.; the 15.3 miles from Tallington to the Summit having taken only 15 mins 45 secs. The most notable feature of the run between

Grantham and York was 57 m.p.h. minimum over Markham Summit after climbing a bank which includes over three miles at 1 in 200.

In assessing the merit of this remarkable performance, the heavy demand on electrical energy, for forced draft ventilation, lavatory water heating, cooking and other purposes, must be taken into account in addition to the 635 ton weight of the train which would equal 19 vehicles of the previous Flying Scotsman stock.

The gains in time were in recovery of late starts, that from King's Cross being 2 minutes late owing to the necessity of attaching extra stock at the last minute, and departure from York was five minutes late owing to three minutes lost by very heavy traffic at that station.

<u>Date: 26/9/38.</u>

| MILES | STATIONS. Etc. | | SCHED. | ACTUAL | SPEEDS |
|---|---|---|---|---|---|
| 5.5 | Beningbrough | ... ... | - | 8 40 | 59 |
| 11.2 | ALNE | ... ... | 14 | 14 08 | 65 |
| 16.1 | Pilmoor | ... ... | - | 18 48 | 63 |
| 22.2 | THIRSK | ... ... | 25 | 24 30 | 66 |
| 30.0 | NORTHALLERTON | ... ... | 32° | 31 43 | 63 |
| 33.7 | Danby Wiske | ... ... | - | 35 13 | 66 |
| 38.9 | ERYHOLME | ... ... | 41 | 39 58 | 64 |
| 41.5 | Croft Spa | ... ... | - | 42 16 | 69 |
| 44.1 | DARLINGTON | ... ... | 46 | 44 40 | 54* |
| 49.5 | Aycliffe | ... ... | - | 50 46 | 52 |
| 54.2 | Bradbury | ... ... | - | 56 11 | 51 |
| 57.0 | FERRYHILL | ... ... | 60° | 58 56 | 66 |
| 61.9 | Croxdale | ... ... | - | 63 35 | - |
| 66.1 | DURHAM | ... ... | 72 | 69 06 | 30* |
| 71.9 | Chester-le-Street | ... ... | - | 75 38 | 69 |
| 74.7 | BIRTLEY | ... ... | 81 | 78 00 | 73 |
| 77.6 | Low Fell | ... ... | - | 80 28 | - |
| 80.1 | NEWCASTLE | ... ... | 90 | 86 00 | - |

*Key to symbols:* ~ Slack for curves. # At milepost 62. * Service slack. « Slack for troughs. S Signals.

For the 1939 season of non-stop running, No.2512 was one of the only three which King's Cross shed needed to use. Here on the Up train it is near Hatfield, with one of the new fourteen-coach air-conditioned sets put into use that year.

Coming south over the Royal Boarder bridge at Berwick No.4482 was one of Haymarket's selected engines for the non-stop running in the 1938 summer. Until 25th February 1938 it was shedded at King's Cross and they had used it on non-stops in 1937.

*(right)* During the winter season of 1938/1939, the Up train is making the call at York and No.4493 has a fifteen coach load to run the 188 miles to London in 193 minutes including a call at Grantham.

*(below)* King's Cross shedded No.4498 was used frequently on the non-stops in the 1938 and 1939 summers and here on the Up train it is at Naburn, between York and Selby. The last pre-war non-stops ran on Saturday 2nd September 1939 with No.4488 on the Down and No.4490 on the Up working.

Throughout the war the *FLYING SCOTSMAN* was one of only three LNER trains to retain its name, but that only appeared in the timetable, as destination indication on trains was forbidden. Twenty-coach loads became usual and the inclusion of many more stops spread running time to 8½ and even 9 hours. Here in 1943 Gateshead's No.4464 is on the Down train.

*(opposite)* Dated 5th April 1943, this view shows an unusual engine working because at that time No.4900 was a Doncaster allocation. Further, the carrying of a roof board by the first coach broke the existing rules.

The coaching stock became much more varied with anything available being used for extra coaches. The second vehicle on this Down train is a clerestory roof type which had been unusual after the stock built in 1924 was introduced.

During 1946 all the LNER locomotives were renumbered; No.7 having originally been No.4498. Here, on 7th April 1947, it has the Down train at Potters Bar with the pre-war headboard and coach roof boards again in use, but calls were made by the Down train at Peterborough, York, Newcastle and Berwick, and the Up train at Newcastle, York and Grantham. Timings were 8 hours 17 minutes Down, and 8 hours 5 minutes by the Up. A through portion to and from Aberdeen was the only addition.

**Post-War Recovery.**

From 31st May 1948 it was possible for the 10 o'clock departures to resume non-stop running for the summer season, but with overall time extended to 7 hours 50 minutes. By then, however, it was the responsibility of British Railways, the LNER having had to succumb to political nationalisation. Traffic was still so heavy that there was also a 9.50 a.m. from King's Cross to Glasgow and a relief to the non-stop *FLYING SCOTSMAN* leaving at 10.05 which made calls at Peterborough, York, Newcastle and Berwick. Grantham was catered for by the 9.50 a.m. which then had Darlington as its next stop. There were corresponding return trains to London.

The first train was given the 'right-away' at King's Cross by the Lord Mayor of London and A4 No.60034 LORD FARINGDON hauled it whilst from Edinburgh, A4 No.60009 UNION OF SOUTH AFRICA brought the Up train. Despite twenty-two corridor type tenders then being available, all were and continued to be, coupled only to A4 class engines which thus monopolised the non-stop workings.

During the night of Tuesday 12th August 1948, some 6¼ inches of rain caused floods which washed away bridges on the main line in Berwickshire and also a landslide at Tynehead blocking use of the alternative Waverley route. On the 13th August the Down intended non-stop, diverted to run via the Waverley route from Carlisle to Edinburgh, had got as far as Hawick before news of the landslide halted its further progress. It returned to Carlisle and then went via Carstairs to reach Edinburgh at 3.51 a.m. the following morning! This seventeen hours and fifty-one minutes journey time gave the train (and its passengers) one more record - that of endurance. The floods also led to an extension of the world non-stop mileage record because by 17th August debris on the Waverley line enabled it to be used between Edinburgh and St Boswells then across through Kelso to join the main line at Tweedmouth and with no reversal required. That was a 408½ mile journey

and some Haymarket drivers prided themselves on being able to ignore a permissible stop for water at St Boswells and run the 90 miles to beyond Belford and then replenish from the track troughs between there and Lucker. This world record for long distance running by steam then stood until 1989 when it was increased to 422 miles but was still held by a Gresley Pacific, none other than the engine FLYING SCOTSMAN during its Australian visit.

As happened in pre-war days it was the non-stop which grabbed the headlines despite the relatively short period of operation each summer. But even as soon after the war as from 1st October 1945, restaurant cars were restored to the train which made calls and its schedule was cut considerably, the Down train reaching Edinburgh at 6.05 p.m., the Up train doing slightly better by getting into London at 6.00 p.m. Both still needed another train running as a relief, at 9.40 from London and 10.15 a.m. from Edinburgh. This pattern continued almost unchanged until after the LNER had ceased to exist.

In the 1949 summer new thinking changed the roles of the main and relief trains, the non-stop with its passengers all perforce making the 392.7 mile journey then being regarded as the relief. This enabled retention of the traditional 10 o'clock departures and *FLYING SCOTSMAN* name. Train naming having become firmly established, that bestowed on the non-stop was *THE CAPITALS LIMITED*, and that train is described separately.

Pre-war *FLYING SCOTSMAN* headboards were brought out again and also used the year round. One of them at least was repainted in Gill sans letters which although adopted as standard by the LNER in 1932 had not been applied to a *FLYING SCOTSMAN* board prior to the war. None of those painted boards ever showed 'The Flying Scotsman' and all had the name in two lines as the 1928 boards were still used to 1939 and then again in 1946 to 1950 when superseded by cast iron plates. Those had beaded edge and the raised letters included 'The' and were in three lines.

Post-war the 10 o'clocks settled down to stopping only at Grantham and Newcastle (where the engine was changed) and to a journey time of around 7½ hours. The Down train had coaches only for Edinburgh, but on the Up working the coaches from Aberdeen were still attached there. What had been the Glasgow portion became a complete restaurant car train from London at 10.05 a.m. and at 8.35 a.m. from Glasgow and 10.10 a.m. out of Waverley. Both made calls at Peterborough, York, Darlington, Durham, Newcastle and Berwick.

With the *FLYING SCOTSMAN* changing engines at Newcastle, it was no longer constrained to using A4 class haulage with corridor tender but that class still took by far the most workings. The remainder were shared by the Peppercorn A1 and A2 classes with occasional use of Gresley V2's.

After Peter Townend took charge at King's Cross shed in 1956 and put new life into the twenty and thirty year old A3 class, these put in many really splendid runs from London to and from Newcastle. The Thompson Pacifics were only used when called on to deputise for a failure such as on 31st July 1959 when York's No.60502 went through Hitchin on the Up train.

From September 1961 it was rare to see a headboard carried by a timetabled train on what had been LNER lines. Monday 18th June 1962 did provide full justification for carrying one. In June 1862, the 'Special Scotch Express' began leaving King's Cross at what was to become the immutable departure time of 10 o'clock. By the 1880's the public had dubbed it "The Flying Scotchman" and by 1893 the railway press described it as known the world over. Recognised officially only in 1924, June 1962 was undoubtedly its centenary.

For the departure on 18th June, 'Top Shed' used a Deltic diesel D9020 NIMBUS in immaculate condition and provided it not only with the 1A16 identity but also a cast headboard with train name and circular plaques. The Lord Mayor of London and the Lord Provost of Edinburgh gave the trains their 'right-away' The Up train's headboard turned the wheel full circle - it was a simple white painted plate with black letters just as Haymarket had used on that memorable day in May 1928.

**Epilogue:**

There was to be just one more "Flying Scotsman" nostalgic memory. On 1st May 1968, restored steam engine No.4472 named FLYING SCOTSMAN successfully hauled a non-stop train to Edinburgh in 7 hours 44 minutes, leaving King's Cross at the traditional time of 10 o'clock. Correctly in line with forty years previously, this non-stop from the London end carried no headboard.

Three days later, No.4472 repeated its non-stop in the other direction, going back to King's Cross in 7 hours 35½ minutes and that really was the end of non-stop running for the FLYING SCOTSMAN train.

Until the end of May 1948, Gateshead shed took a share of the workings between Newcastle and London and used A3 class engines for many of them as here with No.78.

Haymarket shed had responsibility for the locomotives used between Newcastle and Edinburgh, and here, on 3rd April 1948, the Down train is entering Waverley station behind British Railways No.E4. On the headboard note "Flying" is in smaller lettering than "Scotsman". Hitherto the same height of lettering had been used for both words.

*(opposite)* Gateshead's A3 No.76 is representative of the train engine when the LNER ceased to exist on 31st December 1947. Some, but not all, of the 1938 built air-conditioned coaches were again being used. Note that the headboard had different lettering style to that on No.78 in the previous illustration.

On 31st May 1948 it was possible to restore summer non-stop running to the 10 o'clock trains albeit on no better than 7 hours 50 minutes timing. A4 No.60034 took out the first post-war non-stop from King's Cross and No.60009 is at Finsbury Park with the first from Edinburgh.

*(opposite)* A4 No.60028, in the experimental purple/blue paint of 1948, has charge of the non-stop Down train passing through York in the summer of 1948.

*(left)* Due to flood damage washing out seven bridges between Berwick and Dunbar on 13th August 1948, the next three days saw the non-stops diverted from Selby via Leeds, Settle, Carlisle and Carstairs. On the 14th and 16th A4 No.25 took the Down train and is here passing Kirkstall. Stops had to be made to collect and drop conductor drivers familiar with the ex LMS lines then used.

*(below)* By the evening of 16th August 1948, flood debris had been cleared from the Waverley route, enabling the non-stops (and other traffic) to use it as far as St. Boswells. Then via Kelso to the main line, joining and leaving it at Tweedmouth. A stop for water at St. Boswells was authorised but Scottish drivers prided themselves on reaching the troughs at Belford. No.60031 on the Down train is at Falahill summit on the 408$\frac{1}{2}$ mile journey. The last *FLYING SCOTSMAN* non-stops were on 25th September 1948.

(above) In the later months of 1948 Haymarket did not rely entirely on their A4's for going to and from Newcastle on the *FLYING SCOTSMAN* trains. With 156 minutes Up and 160 minutes Down (which included a call at Berwick) for the 124.4 miles, they considered the liberal timing well suited to the 6in. smaller driving wheels of their new A2 class of which they then only had No.E529.

(top right) A2 class were also used on occasion south of Newcastle, because No.60539 of Heaton shed is on the Up train at Finsbury Park. During the four days 10th to 13th May 1949, A1 No.60114 and then on the 17th to the 20th May, A2 No.60539 did high power tests on the Down 'Scotsman' to Grantham, returning with the Up 'Scotsman'. To the normal fourteen coaches, three empties and the dynamometer car were added to give a load of 610/615 tons.

(right) In the winter of 1948/1949, Grantham shed was again responsible for the Down train from London to Newcastle and their A3 No.60039 is accelerating from the call at Darlington. It did this working almost every weekday from 28th February to 11th June 1949.

(above) When the 1949 summer train service began on 23rd May, the non-stop running was transferred to a new train *THE CAPITALS LIMITED*. Meanwhile, *FLYING SCOTSMAN* kept to its 10 o'clock departure from both ends and engines were changed at Newcastle. The Down train - as here five miles north of York - had a Grantham locomotive from London to Newcastle.

(left) From the 1949 summer, the Up *FLYING SCOTSMAN* motive power from Newcastle to London was provided by King's Cross shed and could either be an A4 class as here, or one of the new Peppercorn A1's.

*(right)* In the summer of 1950, King's Cross shedded A1 No.60157 (one of the five with roller bearing axle boxes) has the Up train rounding the curve at Chaloners Whin junction south of York. The Aberdeen portion was carried by this train but the Down train only then had Edinburgh coaches.

*(below)* The Up train entering York on 22nd August 1950 and by that summer its engine from Newcastle to London was provided by Gateshead shed instead of King's Cross shed. Because Gateshead had both A1 and A4 classes allocated, their use of A3 No.60040 was somewhat unusual. This was the last recorded use of a pre-war painted headboard.

*(above)* The cast plates introduced in 1950 then completely superseded the pre-war painted type and on A1 class were usually carried on the upper lamp iron. Here Gateshead's No.60145 is on the Up train at Bishopthorpe, 3 miles south of York.

*(left)* The Down train continued to be worked by King's Cross shed and they used a variety of types, but usually an A4 or an A1 appeared. Here No.60013 has the train taking it from London to Newcastle.

During the Coronation year of 1953, the cast type headboards had plaques applied to them, those on the *FLYING SCOTSMAN* showing an intertwined rose and thistle. Here on the Down train, A1 No.60156 of King's Cross shed is passing through York.

Whilst Gateshead were still working the Up train through to London, A1 No.60147 is here making the Grantham call, and one of the headboard plaques has already gone missing.

*(right)* Starting with the 1955 summer service, the Up working from Newcastle was changed from a Gateshead to a King's Cross shedded engine and on it, A4 No.60022 is just south of Darlington.

*(below)* A4 No.60014 on the Up train on 27th September 1955 is about to run through Peterborough station. Note this headboard still carried both plaques.

*(above)* The adhesive used for the plaques did not stand up to the service required of it, and by July 1959 the headboard here on No.60008, with the Down train at Grantham, was bereft of both its plaques.

*(left)* A4 No.60033 on 27th June 1960 is leaving King's Cross on the Down train and the headboard shows rough removal of both plaques. Both headboard and left hand lamp appear to have been put on hurriedly and the whole appearance of the engine is out of keeping with how Top Shed turned them out for named trains. The A4 looks to be a last minute substitution for the booked engine.

(above) One headboard still retained a single plaque at least to the end of 1960 because Grantham shedded No.60049 did not get these smoke deflectors until it was ex works on 21st October 1960 - the first A3 so fitted. The engine was then sent on loan to King's Cross shed who used it for a week on the Down 10 o'clock as far as Newcastle and back the same day, on what by then was normally a diesel working.

(right) At Grantham in July 1960, No.60022 is about to return to London on a train without a name. Note the headboard used on its outward journey is now reversed. Carried on the lamp iron it would suffer less damage than if loose in the cab. The inscription reads "Return to DMPS King's X".

*(above)* A4 No.60024, of Haymarket shed, worked Up on Saturday 5th August 1961 on the non-stop train *THE ELIZABETHAN* and here, with that headboard reversed, it is returning to Edinburgh on the 10 o'clock from King's Cross on Sunday 6th August. The only calls were at Grantham, York and Newcastle, and there were through coaches to Aberdeen. There was no parallel 10 o'clock Sunday train from Scotland, the equivalent which did not have an Aberdeen portion, left Edinburgh at 10.50 and called at Newcastle, Darlington and Grantham. Neither was a named train.

*(left)* The Up train on Friday 31st July 1959 at Hitchin with A2/2 class No.60502 of York shed. The rostered King's Cross engine from Newcastle must have failed.

*(above)* Occasionally, after it ceased to be a non-stop, King's Cross shed used a V2, as here on Monday 19th September 1955, No.60821 being on the Up train south of Stoke tunnel.

*(right)* The Down train in 1959, about 5 miles north of York. New England V2 No.60869 had taken over from the engine which had left King's Cross, but its driver W. Hoole, had the train back on time by York.

Prior to the cast plates, here is a black painted one with white lettering.

*(opposite)* When the cast headboards came into use, they had a beaded edge and raised letters with a bright face to contrast with the black background.

The start of the *FLYING SCOTSMAN* centenary run - 18th June 1962.

*(right)* Preserved A3 No.4472 passing Durham on 1st May 1968 on the London to Edinburgh non-stop run to mark the 40th anniversary of its inaugural.

*(below)* After the anniversary non-stop run to Edinburgh on 1st May 1968, No.4472 left Waverley on the 4th May at 2.20 p.m. and ran non-stop to King's Cross. Here on that run it is climbing Cockburnspath bank.

From 11th July 1927, the 7.30 p.m. from King's Cross and the 7.15 p.m. from Aberdeen sleeping car expresses were named *ABERDONIAN* but until 1932 no display of name was carried by the train. Here the Down train, due in Aberdeen at 7.30 a.m. is approaching that station, the engines being C10 No.9902 of Dundee and D29 No.9899 of Aberdeen sheds.

# THE ABERDONIAN

Prior to the opening of the Forth Bridge in 1890, overnight through travel between King's Cross and Aberdeen was not easy, and my Great Northern Railway timetable starting 1st August 1880 sets out what was required. *"The Sleeping Carriage which ordinarily runs between London (King's Cross Station GNR) and Perth, can go through to Aberdeen when Four Tickets, at least, are taken to or from Aberdeen, and sufficient notice is given to the Superintendent of the Line (King's Cross Station GNR London), or to the East Coast Company's Agent at Aberdeen for the carriage to be sent to Aberdeen."* This all involved the North British Railway exercising their running powers over the Caledonian Railway metals from Perth to Aberdeen. The 8.30 p.m. departure from King's Cross had an 8.30 a.m. arrival at Perth and did not reach Aberdeen until 12.40 p.m.. In the Up direction, the Aberdeen departure was timed at 4.05 p.m.; Perth was left at 7.35 p.m. for arrival in King's Cross at 8.15 a.m. next morning.

The opening of the Forth Bridge enabled the Aberdeen trains to run via Dundee instead of via Polmont, Stirling and Perth, reducing the North British dependence on running powers over its rival to just the thirty-eight miles north of Kinnaber junction, instead of the ninety miles between Perth and Aberdeen. Even more importantly, the North British remained in charge of the train all the way, instead of having to hand over the coaches at Perth.

The East Coast route now had the advantage where Aberdeen traffic was concerned, and this led to the 'Race' to Aberdeen in 1895, which showed what could be done. On the night of August 21st/22nd the 523.7 miles were run in 506$^{1}/_{2}$ minutes,

and the East Coast train was into Aberdeen at 4.40 a.m.. But who would want to arrive so far north at that time on a winter's morning?

More sensible operation and arrival times were soon adopted. When the LNER inherited this train, it left King's Cross at 7.30 p.m. and arrived at Aberdeen at 7.30 a.m. In the Up direction, the Aberdeen departure was at 7.15 p.m. with a London arrival at 7.35 a.m.

The *ABERDONIAN* name was bestowed on this train from 11th July 1927 but there were also through sleeping cars on it to Fort William, and to Inverness. In addition, restaurant cars were included from London to York, and from Aberdeen to Edinburgh, so its normal loading was at least 500 tons. This was well within the capacity of the Gresley Pacifics on the London to Edinburgh portion, but

not until 1930 did they work north of there, and regularly recourse had to be made to two engines from Waverley, usually a North British Atlantic and a 'Scott' class 4-4-0. It was to eliminate this piloting that the powerful P2 class 2-8-2's was introduced in 1934 and they were set to work on the Edinburgh - Aberdeen section.

In each pre-war summer the traffic warranted the running of two, and sometimes three, trains, so that the Fort William and Inverness portions became a separate train, which also carried an additional sleeping car portion for Nairn. This was named the *HIGHLANDMAN* and will be described later. However, the main Aberdeen train had little relief, for added to it was a sleeping car portion for Elgin and Lossiemouth.

The outbreak of war in 1939 restricted

In the early 1930's an engine change at Dundee was the rule, and here C10 No.9904 has the train between Edinburgh and Dundee at Markinch. Pacifics did not normally work to Aberdeen and then they usually were on the fast meat and fish trains when they did from 1930 onwards.

To eliminate the constant and wasteful piloting of the heavy *ABERDONIAN* trains, in 1934 two Class P2 2-8-2 engines were built to run them. No.2002 on 6th August 1935, is ready in Aberdeen to leave with the Up train. Note the headboard has Gills sans lettering and the coaches each have a roof board with train name.

*continued from page 63./* operation to London - Edinburgh - Aberdeen but every train in both directions was crowded with service personnel. It was regarded of sufficient importance to be one of the very few trains to keep its name, although denuded of the engine headboard and carriage roof boards.

By 1946 the headboard was being carried again, still a white painted one with black letters, but now as *THE ABERDONIAN;* that headboard was duly replaced by the cast type with raised lettering, and from 1952 the cast plates were embellished with circular plaques, showing the arms of London and of Aberdeen. During the 1950s the main train left King's Cross at 7.00 p.m. to arrive in Aberdeen at 6.38 a.m. and the regular second portion followed at 7.15 p.m. with a 3.17 a.m. arrival at Edinburgh and then went on to arrive in Fort William at 9.05 a.m., and with refreshments available from Edinburgh onwards.

When the final *Bradshaw's Guide* was issued in May 1961 it still included *THE ABERDONIAN,* then leaving London at 7.30 p.m. and into Aberdeen at 7.19 a.m. and, still with a sleeping car portion for Fort William. From Aberdeen, the named train left at 7.30 p.m. and on Mondays to Fridays *only* sleeping car passengers were conveyed, the London arrival being at 7.39 a.m. - but by then steam haulage and the practice of carrying a headboard was rapidly fading out.

Even with these powerful engines it was still usual to change engines at Dundee, No.2002 being used by that shed to and from Aberdeen, whilst No.2001 worked between Edinburgh and Dundee. Its home shed was Haymarket where it is in this view.

*(right)* From the London end an A4 was usually used for what was a 500 ton load. In addition to the Aberdeen sleeping cars, there were also sleepers for Inverness and for Fort William attached south of Edinburgh. This was one of the three trains which kept its name during the war, but not on the train. No.2512's headboard belonged to King's Cross shed and shows the slight difference in lettering to the more carefully done Scottish version.

*(left)* Carrying of the headboard was resumed in 1946 but showing *THE ABERDONIAN*. Here, passing Brookman's Park on 5th July 1948, King's Cross shed have provided V2 No.909 for it. The Fort William portion was still included but that for Inverness was not resumed post-war.

*(below)* From 1950 the painted headboards were replaced by cast type with raised letters and beaded edges. Here passing Potters Bar on 18th August 1953, King's Cross have provided the roller bearing type A1 No.60157 to work the train to Newcastle.

Backing out from King's Cross station on 16th May 1952, Grantham's A1 No.60128 has brought in *THE ABERDONIAN*. This was the earliest date on which the addition of plaques was noted, in this case depicting the arms of London and of Aberdeen.

From 1932 to 1939 the summer traffic needed a relief train which ran fifteen minutes ahead of the main *ABERDONIAN* train. Named *HIGHLANDMAN* it took the sleeping car portions for Inverness, Nairn and Fort William, allowing the main train to add sleepers for Elgin and Lossiemouth. Coming south the *HIGHLANDMAN* was due into King's Cross five minutes after the Aberdeen train, but that service, and the train name, ceased from the 1939 summer.

# HIGHLANDMAN & NIGHT SCOTSMAN

Officially given the name from 11th July 1927, the *HIGHLANDMAN* ran only in the summer season, and it was 1932 before a headboard was carried. It was essentially a relief train to the *ABERDONIAN* which it preceded by fifteen minutes out of King's Cross, taking the sections for Fort William, for Inverness and for Nairn.

In the 1939 summer, the *HIGHLANDMAN* left King's Cross at 7.25 p.m., had a restaurant car as far as York and arrived in Edinburgh at 3.35 a.m. and there (still just fifteen minutes ahead of the Aberdeen train) it split. The Fort William sleeper portion did not depart until 4.28 a.m. to go via Cowlairs and the West Highland line to arrive in Fort William at 9.22 a.m. Meanwhile the cars for Inverness and Nairn had left Waverley at 3.48 a.m, non-stop to Perth, where an LMS locomotive took over, and a restaurant car was added to provide breakfasts. Inverness was reached at 8.45 a.m. In the opposite direction, departures were 4.40 p.m. from Inverness and 5.10 p.m. from Fort William, to arrive next morning into King's Cross at 7.30 a.m. This train name ceased to be used when war broke out and it was never restored.

What the *ABERDONIAN* meant to Aberdeen and the Highlands, was equalled by the *NIGHT SCOTSMAN* to Edinburgh and district. It generated so much traffic that by LNER days it too regularly needed two separate trains. Official naming stemmed from 11th July 1927 and an engine headboard was added from 1932, but curiously was applied only to the train from London until after the war, when timetables included the belated recognition of the corresponding Up train.

This overnight sleeper service was of long establishment and makes interesting reading in the Great Northern Railway August 1880 timetable. Pride of place is given to a Pullman sleeping car on it, which was "well ventilated, fitted with separate lavatories for Ladies and Gentlemen, and accompanied by a Special Attendant". In addition, there were sleeping carriages of the East Coast Companies, provided with rugs, etc. and fitted with lavatories. For ladies travelling alone, a separate saloon was reserved. The Pullman cars were *Columba* and *Iona*. The Down train left at 9.00 p.m. and arrived in Edinburgh at 7.20 a.m. and the Up left Edinburgh at 10.20 p.m. to arrive King's Cross at 8.15 a.m.

When the LNER came into being on 1st January 1923, Pullman sleeping cars had long been discarded and the amount of traffic required two trains. The first left King's Cross at 10.25 p.m. and had sleeping cars for Glasgow, Dundee and Perth; this was the train to which the name was given in 1927. It was followed at 10.35 p.m. by a sleeping car train just for Edinburgh. To London, Edinburgh passengers had their own sleeper leaving at 10.10 p.m., followed at 10.30 p.m. by the combined train with sleepers from Inverness, Perth and Dundee.

By 1932 the *NIGHT SCOTSMAN* "would only convey passengers for stations beyond Edinburgh" passengers for that city having their own 'first class' and 'third class' sleepers on the 10.35 p.m. from King's Cross. Both trains, in each direction, were heavy and usually of around fourteen vehicles, of which about half were sleeping cars, and it was for such loads that the Gresley Pacifics were multiplied by new building in the period from 1923 to 1925.

Throughout the war, two trains each way were still needed, although they were cut back to London - Edinburgh. The one that had carried the name left London at 10.15 p.m. and was due in Waverley at 7.42 a.m., only thirty-seven minutes slower than in peacetime. The relief did even better, leaving at 10.00 p.m. to arrive in Waverley at 6.57 a.m., only seven minutes longer than pre-war timings.

From October 1946 the Up train at last was named *THE NIGHT SCOTSMAN;* it left Edinburgh at 10.00 p.m., Newcastle at 12.49 a.m., and then ran non-stop to King's Cross for arrival at 6.20 a.m. The relief, with a sleeping car from Dundee, left Edinburgh at 10.20 p.m., called at Newcastle, York and Grantham and was into London at 6.50 a.m. *THE NIGHT SCOTSMAN* from London departed at 10.15 p.m., with sleeping cars for Edinburgh and Dundee, followed by the relief train at 10.30 p.m. In the last *Bradshaw* issue of May 1961, these London departures applied only on Saturdays; on the other nights, the named train did not leave until 11.35 p.m., catering for sleeping car passengers only to Edinburgh, where they arrived at 7.26 a.m. - thus continuing its record as a named train of immense importance, through to the end of haulage by steam.

(opposite) *NIGHT SCOTSMAN* in 1932 or 1933, five minutes before leaving King's Cross, behind Grantham's No.2560. From 1946 the name became *THE NIGHT SCOTSMAN* and in 1950 cast type headboards were introduced. No evidence has been seen that plaques were put on them.

Known from its start, on 9th July 1923, by the name *HARROGATE PULLMAN*, its termini were King's Cross and Newcastle. Nothing was carried on either the engine or the cars but the name was used in advertising. The 185.6 miles London to and from Leeds (Central) was run non-stop, initially by C1 class from King's Cross shed whose No.1459 is arriving at Leeds on the opening day. There the train reversed and was taken forward by an NE Area Atlantic.

# HARROGATE PULLMAN;
# HARROGATE-EDINBURGH PULLMAN; QUEEN OF SCOTS

The LNER took its first step towards train naming on 9th July 1923, when a Pullman service began, connecting King's Cross and Newcastle via Leeds and Harrogate. Although given the name of *HARROGATE PULLMAN*, from the outset it ran forward from that spa, to call at Ripon and Darlington, before terminating at Newcastle.

At Grouping, the new Company found that one of its constituents - the Great Eastern Railway - had an agreement with the Pullman Car Co. which had a considerable period still to run. In addition to the cars which that line included in its Harwich boat trains, it also operated some in its ordinary service trains between Liverpool Street and Norwich, Cromer, Cambridge, Hunstanton, Ipswich and Lowestoft. Those in the Continental boat trains were profitable; decidedly not so in the ordinary services, so that use ceased with the demise of the GER at the end of 1922. To fulfil the agreement, the LNER had to find some way of using the cars and its first step was to transfer them from the GE to the GN Section. The next step was to cease using separate cars in the ordinary expresses, but to introduce trains comprised wholly of Pullman cars, and have confidence that supplementary fares would be acceptable. Then likely routes to run such a train had to be selected, and London - Harrogate looked to have potential, which probably explains the choice of name, even when the train was to go on to Newcastle, and the return service began there. So, with the official name of *HARROGATE PULLMAN*, a Monday to Saturday service in both directions began on 9th July 1923.

The Down train left King's Cross at 11.15 a.m. and ran non-stop to Leeds (Central) the 185.6 miles taking 205 minutes, which equalled the best time so far operated between the two cities. It was also then the LNER's longest non-stop run. At Leeds the train reversed to go via the Bramhope tunnel to Harrogate, reached at 3.15 p.m. then, it called at Ripon and Darlington before terminating in Newcastle at 5.00 p.m. The Up train left Newcastle at 9.20 a.m., made the same calls, left Leeds at 11.50 a.m. and was into King's Cross at 3.15 p.m. This service therefore needed two trains, each of two First and four Third Class cars, and the First's on the inaugural down run were Arcadia and Ansonia, both transferred from the GER. Almost immediately the trains were changed to new stock, cars named Fortuna, Iolanthe, Irene and Rosemary coming from Midland Carriage & Wagon Co., whilst Clayton Wagons of Lincoln supplied the eight Third Class cars. The total cost was £70,000 but keep in mind that the London-Harrogate supplementary fare was six shillings - today's 30 pence!

Each six car set provided 44 First and 132 Third Class seats, and one of them was used for a Press train to Harrogate on Saturday 30th June, with an overnight stay at the Majestic Hotel, and return to London on the Sunday.

With a tare weight of around 250 tons, these trains were ideal for Atlantic type engines to operate, C1 class to and from Leeds, and C7 class north of there. However, the LNER had appointed W.G.P. Maclure as Locomotive Running Superintendent of its Southern Area and he had occupied a similar job

through the whole of the Great Central's twenty-five years. Promoted by the LNER in April 1923, he thought that the GC's most impressive engines, the 4-cylinder 4-6-0 class which became B3, could well be used on the non-stops to and from Leeds. Around the end of July 1923, three of them, Nos.1165, 1166 and 1167, still in full GCR livery, moved from Gorton to King's Cross shed and by August 1924, all six of them were on the GN Section. They were steadier riders than C1 Atlantic's but the best that could be said for them was that their Pullman work was patchy and by 1927 they had all returned to their home ground.

The *HARROGATE PULLMAN* proved a success and encouraged getting remunerative work from the additional cars which the LNER had inherited. After two futile efforts, from 21st September 1925, two sets of cars began to serve Leeds and Bradford, a service which first became the *WEST RIDING PULLMAN* and later, the *YORKSHIRE PULLMAN*. These trains are described later under those names. Meanwhile, from Monday 13th July 1925, the *HARROGATE PULLMAN* had been extended from Newcastle to Berwick and Edinburgh. The Down train timings were the same to Newcastle, and Edinburgh was reached at 7.50 p.m. but the Up timings were appreciably earlier. Departures from Edinburgh at 8.30 a.m. and 11.25 a.m. from Newcastle, and 1.40 p.m. from Leeds, gave a King's Cross arrival at 5.05 p.m. The introduction of the Leeds and Bradford service enabled the *HARROGATE PULLMAN* to better justify its name because from 21st September 1925, it ran non-stop

On one day early in November 1924, the booked engine for the Down train had failed so A1 No.1477N was substituted as seen here at Wood Green. It was detached at Doncaster because Pacifics were not allowed to work to Leeds from Doncaster until 18th July 1930. Initially of six cars, note it had now been increased to eight.

*(opposite)* In the last week of July 1923 the Southern Area Running Superintendent (an ex GC man) arranged for two B3 class emgines to be transferred to King's Cross shed for this Pullman working to and from Leeds. Here at Retford North, on 3rd September 1923, No.1165 still in full Great Central livery has the Up Pullman.

*(above)* Before the GC engines were introduced, King's Cross shed used various GN Atlantics on its allocation for this Pullman working, No.1421 having the Up train approaching Potters Bar. Until into 1924, the six cars ran with an ordinary brake van at each end.

*(left)* Another King's Cross C1 No.1444 here has the Down train in 1923 near Peterborough, whilst bogie brake vans of ordinary stock were still being used.

*(opposite)* By 1924 the train's appearance had been much improved by the Pullman Car Co. providing brake-third cars, which also added to the seats available. By August 1924 all six of the B3 class engines were on the GN section and taking part in the Pullman working to and from Leeds. No.6167 is heading for Wood Green tunnel with the Down *HARROGATE PULLMAN*.

*continued from page 73./* over the 198.8 miles between King's Cross and Harrogate and also eliminated the reversal in Leeds (Central). That was achieved by leaving the East Coast main line at Shaftholme Junction 4½ miles north of Doncaster then traversing ten miles of LMS metals to Knottingley where the LNER Sheffield to York line was joined from which it diverged at Church Fenton to go via Wetherby and on to Harrogate. The ex-GC 4-6-0's took no part in the Pullman workings by this route leaving it mainly to King's Cross based C1's, but from mid-February 1927, Class D11 Nos.5506, 5507 and 5511 were used alternatively. On 26th August 1927, the first Pacific (No.2561) worked from King's Cross to Harrogate because a Royal saloon carrying Queen Mary was added to the usual six Pullmans.

Advertised from July 1927 as the *HARROGATE-EDINBURGH PULLMAN* that was short-lived because from 1st May 1928, further change was made. Two new trains, of all-steel coaches, began working and another extension to Glasgow (Queen Street) made the journey 450.8 miles. The Harrogate title was dropped in favour of the more impressive *QUEEN OF SCOTS* and the service reverted to the call, and reversal, in Leeds. Adjusting the timings found enough response to warrant the Leeds-London service having two Pullmans each way, every day.

The 11.15 a.m. departure from London was retained as was the 205 minute non-stop run to Leeds, also the arrival times at the other call through to Edinburgh and Glasgow was reached at 8.45 p.m. The Up train left Queen Street at 10.05 a.m., Waverley at 11.15 a.m. and Leeds at 4.14 p.m. to arrive in King's Cross at 7.35 p.m. The extension to Glasgow enabled engines of the former NBR to participate and their Atlantics from Haymarket shed were customary although D30 'Scott' class 4-4-0's based at St. Margarets shed also took part, in the workings between the two Scottish cities.

Following the end of the agreed minimum of 8¼ hours for Anglo-Scottish services, from 1932 there was progressive speeding up of the *QUEEN OF SCOTS* timings. By the 1939 summer, the non-stop 185.8 miles were being run in 191 minutes, and Edinburgh was reached at 7.05 p.m. and Glasgow at 8.13 p.m. The Up train left Glasgow at 10.15 a.m. and was in London at 7.05 p.m. The accelerations and the normally fully loaded trains required the margin of power possessed by Pacifics and classes A1, A3 and A4 were all used, even into and out of Glasgow.

When the 1932 summer service started on 18th July, a headboard showing the trains' name was provided, with sharply contrasting use of it south, and north of Leeds. On the GN Section it was as rare for it to be missing as it was for one to be seen on the NE and NB sections. Tradition on the North Eastern Railway gave no encouragement to such frills, understandable when their top lamp iron to carry one was above the smokebox on their engines. At speed, that could be a precarious position, and it also interfered with smoke clearance from the chimney, by almost masking it. The reversal at Leeds also involved a change of engine, and it seems to have been too much for NE men to collect the board, walk the length of the train, and put it on their own engine. Equally the GN men regarded the headboard as the property of King's Cross shed, and that they would need it for the return working. Some effort to improve on this took effect in 1936, when a longer, shallower headboard in a single line name, began to be seen north of Leeds and the change to Pacific haulage also helped because their top lamp iron was mounted on the smokebox door so there was no masking of the chimney and the lower level also made putting it on that much easier for the fireman.

The 1939-45 war caused the cessation of all the Pullman trains from 2nd September 1939 and the *QUEEN OF SCOTS* never ran again as an LNER responsibility. When restarted, on 5th July 1948,

British Railways had taken over and between London and Leeds it became a ten-car train with a gross load of around 500 tons, although only eight cars were taken north of Leeds. At first, both the pre-war headboard types were brought out and carried and with increased enthusiasm north of Leeds. The running times could not yet match those of pre-war, and leaving King's Cross at 11.20 a.m. it took until 9.22 p.m. to get into Glasgow (Queen Street). The Up train left Glasgow at 10.15 a.m. to arrive in London at 8.10 p.m.

From 1950 the headboards were superseded by cast plates with a beaded edge and raised letters with polished face. They also made a slight change to the train's title, which then became *THE QUEEN OF SCOTS* and they continued to be carried until the late 1950's but were then discarded even by the Eastern Region.

Serving the same places, the 1952 Down train left King's Cross at 12.05 p.m. ran non-stop to Leeds in 195 minutes and had 7.52 p.m. and 9.02 p.m. arrivals in Edinburgh and Glasgow respectively. The Up train left Glasgow at 10.50 a.m. and completed its journey in London at 7.50 p.m. By 1961, the overall times had been eased out by about twenty minutes, the Down train taking from 11.50 a.m. to 9.10 p.m. and the Up left Glasgow at 11.00 a.m. and was due in King's Cross at 8.20 p.m. With their typical cynicism at this deterioration, in 1964 British Railways announced that improvements which had been made on the main line had caused passengers north of Leeds to switch to the direct trains and that the Pullman train *THE QUEEN OF SCOTS* would cease to run after Saturday 13th June 1964. Between Leeds and London, that section of it would be replaced by a *WHITE ROSE PULLMAN* for which, refer to its description under "THE WHITE ROSE" heading.

B3 class No.6168 worked on the *HARROGATE PULLMAN* for exactly a year - from April 1924 to April 1925, and during that time it had a large GCR style number plate but with LNER 6168 on it. All the B3 class ceased work on the Pullmans in February 1927 and went back to the GC Section.

On Monday 13th July 1925, this Pullman was extended from Newcastle to Berwick and Edinburgh and then on 21st September 1925 began to run the 198.8 miles direct to Harrogate, cutting out the reversal in Leeds (Central). From Shaftholme junction it went to Knottingley, Church Fenton and Wetherby, as the Up train is seen here between Tadcaster and Church Fenton. Note the coach roof boards put on to show HARROGATE-EDINBURGH PULLMAN.

When the engines were changed at Leeds, and from 21st September 1925 at Harrogate, Heaton C7 class had the train to and from Newcastle. No.2196 of Gateshead shed is making the Ripon call with the Up train. At that period the normal load was six cars which was well within the capabilities of C7 class. When the train was extended to Edinburgh, Gateshead shed also worked that leg from and to Newcastle.

*(opposite)* From early 1927 when the GC 4-6-0's were sent back to that section, haulage to and from King's Cross reverted to that shed's C1 class. A change of title to *HARROGATE-EDINBURGH PULLMAN* began to be used in press advertising in July 1927 to tie-up with the name on the train.

Considerable change took place, effective 1st May 1928. Two new 8-car sets of all-steel construction were introduced, the name became *QUEEN OF SCOTS*, the call and reversal at Leeds was resumed, and the service was extended to Glasgow (Queen Street). Between there and Edinburgh, Haymarket engines were used. D30 class No.9409 is traversing Princes Street Gardens with the train from Glasgow in the 1928/1929 winter. The new name permitted use of  much shorter roof boards.

In 1928 Gateshead still had the working of the Edinburgh-Newcastle section and here their C6 No.1753 on a new eight car set seems to have been halted by signals at Drem station. It made a call there to encourage traffic to and from North Berwick.

(right) For Edinburgh-Glasgow and return, Haymarket used a variety of classes. Here in 1929 summer, their C11 class No.9877 is approaching Waverley station through Princes Street Gardens.

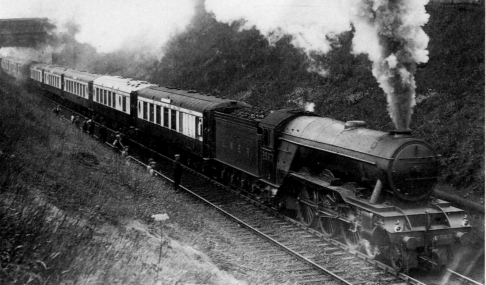

*(above)* At sometime after May 1929, the Gateshead engine for the Edinburgh-Newcastle run must have been 'not available' and Haymarket's C7 No.2193 was substituted instead.

*(left)* From 1929, the building of additional Gresley Pacifics enabled the earlier ones to be drafted on to workings such as the *QUEEN OF SCOTS*. Here, in 1929 Haymarket A1 No.2567 is climbing the 1 in 41$\frac{1}{2}$ Cowlairs incline from Glasgow (Queen Street) with banking assistance at the rear of the train.

*(opposite)* Here, in May 1932 near Darlington, Gateshead shed have used No.2402 one of their five A2 class Raven Pacifics on the *QUEEN OF SCOTS* from Newcastle to Leeds (Central). For this trip, one of the eight cars has not been included.

On 10th June 1930, and before its official release to the Traffic Department on the 21st, the experimental high pressure engine No.10000 took the *QUEEN OF SCOTS* to Leeds, from Newcastle as seen here about to set off.

In May 1932 an engine headboard was introduced. It was used regularly by the GN Section, occasionally in Scottish Area but only very rarely in the North Eastern Area. Their aversion to headboards persisted until into British Railways days. King's Cross shedded C1's were concentrated on working the *WEST RIDING PULLMAN* so a Pullman link was established at Leeds Copley Hill to work the *QUEEN OF SCOTS* to and from London in 191 minutes for the 185.8 miles, and the standard formation was seven cars which No.3280 has.

The Leeds Pullman link was made up of only three engines, Nos.3280, 4423 and 4433, with three sets of men, who each kept to their own engine. Here No.4423 on the Down train is passing Grantham. In 1935, No.4460 and its crew moved from King's Cross to Leeds to strengthen the link. At the end of October 1936 loads and speeds required haulage by Pacifics and two of them were then based at Leeds.

Until 1934 the five Raven A2 Pacifics were still shedded at Gateshead and that shed occasionally used them on the *QUEEN OF SCOTS* from Edinburgh to Newcastle as No.2401 is here, leaving Waverley. The NE Area's dislike of a headboard can be understood from its protruding position due to Darlington designs having the upper lamp iron above the smokebox. But instead of sensibly moving the iron on to the door (where it would also have been easier to reach) they jibbed at using headboards.

*(above)* In 1931, Raven Pacific No.2402 is here coasting through the Leeds suburbs in the Headingley/Kirkstall area. This was prior to a headboard being introduced for this Pullman train.

*(above, right)* By 1933, Heaton shed had replaced Gateshead for working the *QUEEN OF SCOTS* between Newcastle and Leeds. Their usual choice was one of their three A1 class Nos.2579, 2581 or 2582 and with the Down train, No.2581 is here nearing Darlington.

*(right)* The line between Leeds and Harrogate was far from easy, and out of Leeds (Central) it was a stiff climb to Holbeck and then a sharp curve on to the Midland line from which it was up hill all the way to the 2 miles 24.3 yards Bramhope tunnel. Then, to reach Harrogate the 90° curve had to be taken at Crimple Junction which No.2582 is negotiating here in 1938. Even in 1939, twenty-nine minutes had to be allowed for that 18$\frac{1}{4}$ miles, and twenty-eight minutes from Harrogate to Leeds.

Heaton's No.2579, here at Headingley on 12th February 1938, shows the effort needed to take the *QUEEN OF SCOTS* out of Leeds to Harrogate. Despite the lamp iron on the smokebox door, an aversion in the NE Area to carrying headboard persisted.

*(above)* On 4th May 1934, Heaton's 2579 and 2581 were both in works for general repair so C7 class No.2197 was sent for the Pullman and Leeds Neville Hill shed had to provide assistance from Leeds to Harrogate with D49 class No.273. Here the pair are at Headingley.

*(left)* B17 class No.2872 was brand new from Robert Stephenson & Co. in July 1937, and whilst doing acceptance trials before its initial allocation to Gorton, it found its way on to working the *QUEEN OF SCOTS* from Leeds to Newcastle and here is approaching Croft Spa.

*(opposite, top)* In the early 1930's, the job from Edinburgh to Newcastle was a Gateshead Pacific working, and on it A1 No.2569, here is at Portobello and carrying the headboard.

*(opposite)* The Up train from Newcastle to Leeds was also worked by Gateshead and No.2569, again with headboard, here on 25th June 1937 is at Low Fell.

*(left)* Gateshead shed's A4 No.4499 with original naming but without a train headboard is coasting through Headingley on its way to Central station with the Up *QUEEN OF SCOTS* on Saturday 30th April 1938.

*(opposite)* One of Gateshead's A1 class has been through to Glasgow (Queen Street) and here on 4th August 1938 has the Up *QUEEN OF SCOTS* in Princes Street Gardens, Edinburgh. No.2574 would almost certainly take the train on to Newcastle.

*(below)* At the end of 1936 an alternative headboard appeared which was longer and less deep, and on which Gill sans lettering was used. It was carried only rarely pre-war, but survived to be used from King's Cross shed in 1948. Here on 1st January 1937 at Low Fell, Gateshead A3 No.2503 is taking the *QUEEN OF SCOTS* to Leeds from Newcastle.

When only five weeks old, Gateshead A4 No.4469, here at Low Fell on 7th May 1938, is on the Up *QUEEN OF SCOTS* to Leeds from Newcastle. It has one of the 1932 short, deep, headboards on which all three words had the same depth of lettering.

Here at Low Fell, on 12th April 1939, Haymarket A3 No.2508 is working the *QUEEN OF SCOTS* through from Edinburgh to Leeds, but without carrying a headboard.

Strengthening of a bridge over the river Calder south of Wakefield in 1936 permitted the regular use of Pacifics between Doncaster and Leeds (Central). In the last week of October 1936, two A1 Class engines moved to Leeds Copley Hill shed, specifically to work the *QUEEN OF SCOTS* to and from London in 190 minutes for the 185.8 miles. Here in 1937 leaving King's Cross, No.2555 has the Down train. The other A1 was No.2553.

*(above)* After 2nd September 1939, the war caused cancellation of the *QUEEN OF SCOTS* Pullman. When resumption was possible on 5th July 1948, the name was modified to *THE QUEEN OF SCOTS* and British Railways had taken over. It still ran through to Glasgow and reversed in Leeds (Central) but in 1948 from Newcastle to Leeds the Up train had a B1 from Leeds Neville Hill shed, No.1259 here being just south of Darlington. Note the North Eastern Region also dodged carrying a headboard.

*(left)* One of the deep, narrow 1932 headboards had been repainted in the pre-war period with the thinner Gill sans type letters and with the middle word painted much smaller, then the long, shallow headboard was similarly treated. The lamp iron on the smokebox door gave an ideal mounting position in LNER days but problems arose in BR days. Between London and Leeds, rarely was the engine seen without a headboard and both the short, deep and the long, shallow pre-war types reappeared. To and from London to Leeds ten cars were now normal loading which required Pacific haulage, as here in 1948 with A3 class 60104 about to leave Leeds. The fitting of a smokebox numberplate put the lamp iron higher and had a detrimental effect on the headboard position.

*(above)* By 1949 five of the new powerful Peppercorn A1 class engines were at Leeds Copley Hill shed to work to and from King's Cross. Here No.60118 is coming out of Leeds (Central) for London with the *QUEEN OF SCOTS* carrying pre-war headboards.

*(above, right)* For the first Down train on 5th July 1948, King's Cross provided the 1936 long, shallow headboard which did not sit quite so well on the higher lamp iron of A3 class No.60107.

*(right)* First evidence of the modified name and new headboard style was this December 1949 photograph of Eastfield B1 No.61064 entering Waverley station from Glasgow.

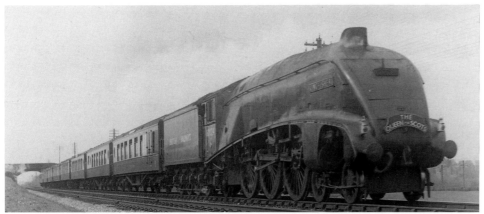

*(left)* From Edinburgh as far as Newcastle, the responsibility for the train was Haymarket's and an A4 was their usual provision, as here with No.60024. They took no chances with the headboard using the centre lamp iron above the buffer beam.

*(below)* In the other direction in the 1951 summer, Gateshead A1 No.60154 has the Newcastle to Edinburgh section of the down train on Cockburnspath Bank. It is crossing one of the replacement bridges put in after the floods of August 1947 washed away the original. The lower headboard position was unusual on A1 class.

*(right)* Use of V2 class on *THE QUEEN OF SCOTS* was most exceptional, but here in June 1950, one shedded at Peterborough is passing Croft Spa and working it from Newcastle to Leeds, as the rostered Leeds Neville Hill engine was not available.

*(below)* Ultimately the two Leeds sheds worked both trains south of Newcastle, Neville Hill between there and Leeds, whilst Copley Hill dealt with the Leeds-London section. Here, on 1st November 1958 at New Southgate, Copley Hill's A1 No.60131 is working from London to Leeds and this is the last time this headboard was noted being carried. No additional plaques were applied to the headboards for *THE QUEEN OF SCOTS.*

*(below, right)* Here in 1959, Neville Hill's A3 No.60036 is on the Down train coming out of Leeds (Central) and at Three Signal Box Junction is diverging to run at the side of the Midland line for 53 chains to Wortley North Junction, before turning North to climb to Bramhope tunnel and on to Harrogate.

Copley Hill A1 No.60134 is pulling out of Leeds (Central) for King's Cross.

Immaculate A1 No.60118, also of Copley Hill, is at Wortley South Junction on its way to London circa 1959. By April 1962 the headboard was no longer carried even on the GN Section. *THE QUEEN OF SCOTS* ran for the last time on Saturday 13th June 1964.

A3 No.60086 of Neville Hill shed here at Wortley North taking it on to Newcastle.

In place of a Neville Hill engine, Heaton A1 No.60116 is pulling out of Leeds (Central) for Newcastle.

The inaugural run of the *SHEFFIELD PULLMAN* was on 2nd June 1924 with King's Cross C1 class No.4426 doing the outward trip and here making the call at Nottingham (Victoria) on the way back to London. No indication of the official name of the train was carried.

# SHEFFIELD PULLMAN; MANCHESTER PULLMAN; WEST RIDING PULLMAN; YORKSHIRE PULLMAN

## SHEFFIELD PULLMAN

Although the introduction of the all-Pullman train to Harrogate in July 1923 absorbed some of the stock from the Great Eastern Railway, more cars were still available, and the success of their first Pullman encouraged the LNER to consider where others might be used to advantage. Sheffield was thought to have Pullman potential despite its well-established services to Marylebone and to St.Pancras. So, on Monday 2nd June 1924, at 11.05 a.m., newly superheated C1 No.4426 left King's Cross with one First and four Third Class Pullman cars. Just North of Grantham it left the main line to call at Nottingham (Victoria) from 1.28 to 1.32 p.m. and then reach Sheffield (Victoria) at 2.20 p.m. After servicing, it returned from Sheffield at 4.45 p.m. called at Nottingham and was back in King's Cross at 8.00 p.m. Known officially as the *SHEFFIELD PULLMAN*, neither engine nor train carried any indication of it.

It quickly became apparent that there was more interest from railway enthusiasts in this train than by those prepared to pay to ride in it. The working was shared by King's Cross and Gorton sheds, and on arrival at Sheffield No.4426 took an ordinary train on to Manchester, where the London crew lodged overnight. Meanwhile, a Gorton engine and crew had worked a Manchester to Sheffield train before they left on the 4.45 p.m. to London, where they lodged before returning on the following morning's Pullman. For the first Up train, Gorton used B2 class No.425c CITY OF MANCHESTER whose arrival in

London was a surprise and a delight to the spotters, who only expected another C1 Atlantic. The B2 did four round trips, and was then seen no more on the Pullman. Actually, it was due for a general repair and by 21st June was in Gorton works. On 11th June, B3 class No.1164c EARL BEATTY took over, and did four return trips from London as it was then at King's Cross shed for working on the *HARROGATE PULLMAN*. Gorton shed sent one more engine on this Pullman working, D10 class No.437c PRINCE GEORGE, arriving in London on the 9th July but meanwhile, King's Cross C1's were used both by their own and Gorton crews. The latter ceased to have any part in this working from Saturday 12th July and by then it was clear this train was not attracting enough patronage even to cover the cost of operating it.

From Monday 14th July, the journeys were reversed. The Up train left Sheffield at 10.30 a.m. called at Nottingham and reached King's Cross at 1.45 p.m. returning thence at 6.05 p.m., made the Nottingham call and was into Sheffield at 9.20 p.m. That did not fare any better!

## MANCHESTER PULLMAN

On 1st April 1925 the Sheffield working was altered to travel via Retford and extended onward to Manchester (Central); although now known as the MANCHESTER PULLMAN, no indication was carried.

Departure was 9.50 a.m. from Manchester, 11.03 a.m. from Sheffield to arrive 2.00 p.m. in

London. The return at 6.05 p.m. was retained and after calling at Sheffield, Manchester arrival was at 10.12 p.m. King's Cross men and C1 class No.4440 worked Down the first day and back the next, but Gorton shedded engines were often seen on it in King's Cross, Nos.5424 and 5425 of B2 class, and 5433, 5437 and 5438 of D10 class being recorded. This service also failed to generate sufficient traffic, so defeat had to be accepted, and from Saturday 19th September 1925, Manchester, Sheffield and Nottingham had no Pullman train.

## WEST RIDING PULLMAN

The next effort to find profitable work for these Pullman cars proved far more successful, rewarding and durable. From 21st September 1925, two Pullman trains were added to the timetable and two sets of cars were needed to work them.

From King's Cross, one left at 11.10 a.m. and ran non-stop to reach Leeds (Central) at 2.35 p.m. where two cars went on to Bradford (Exchange) to arrive at 3.00 p.m. For the Up direction, the cars left at Leeds were taken empty to Harrogate and then formed an 11.15 a.m. departure the following day. On 19th September D21 class was transferred from York to Starbeck shed for this Pullman job to and from Leeds (Central). At Leeds the cars from Harrogate were joined by the two which had left Bradford at 11.20 a.m. and departing at 11.50 a.m. the train ran non-stop to reach London at 3.15 p.m. However, it was not until 1st January 1927 that it was officially named the *WEST RIDING PULLMAN*.

Until Saturday 12th July 1924 the working in each direction alternated between King's Cross and Gorton shedded engines. From the latter, B2 class No.425c did the first four round trips and here on its 3rd June return trip, it is leaving Nottingham (Victoria) for Sheffield.

After 12th July 1924, Gorton engines and crew took no further part in this Pullman working. It was taken entirely by King's Cross C1 class engines as here in August 1924 with No.3301 on the Down working.

Until February 1925 this King's Cross C1 kept its original number 1459 and first L&NER initials. Here on an Up *SHEFFIELD PULLMAN*, it is making the call at Nottingham (Victoria) where the crew get a chance to top-up with water and tend to the coal.

On 1st April 1925 this was altered to become the *MANCHESTER PULLMAN*, calling only at Sheffield (Victoria). Here on 11th June 1925, No.4459 runs through Peterborough with the Up train, as C1 class from King's Cross shed usually worked it.

*continued from page 105./* This extra Pullman service took the Leeds and Bradford passengers from the Harrogate-Edinburgh Pullman (as described in dealing with that train) which was then diverted from Leeds and ran non-stop to Harrogate. After exactly a year, running to the times mentioned above, a call at Wakefield (Westgate) was inserted into the *WEST RIDING PULLMAN* schedule, and the Bradford cars were worked from and to there, avoiding reversal in Leeds. Instead, they went on to service Halifax.

The Wakefield stop made the Leeds arrival time five minutes later, but Bradford's was five minutes earlier, and that portion terminated in Halifax at 3.24 p.m. Next day, those two cars left Halifax at 11.08 a.m., Bradford at 11.35 a.m. and at Wakefield, joined the 11.50 a.m. ex Leeds (which had started from Harrogate at 11.15 a.m.), the Wakefield stop also causing a five-minute later arrival in London. These timings were then retained until the end of April 1928. Now serving three towns and two cities in the West Riding of Yorkshire, the train justified its name.

Starting 1st May 1928, there was a radical change to the timing of the Down train, making this Pullman considerably more attractive to business passengers, and it also needed only one instead of two sets of cars. It also avoided two Pullmans leaving King's Cross only ten minutes apart, and keeping that interval for a distance of 156 miles. The Up train times only altered slightly; it now left Harrogate at 11.00 a.m, Halifax at 10.53 a.m., Bradford at 11.20 a.m., Leeds at 11.35 a.m., and Wakefield at 11.57 a.m. and was then non-stop to arrive King's Cross at 3.00 p.m. After cleaning and servicing, that set of cars could provide the Down train for its departure at 4.45 p.m. and it was into all its three calls and two terminals before 9 o'clock, also giving Harrogate the benefit of a late afternoon service.

With this altered arrangement, from 9th July 1928, it proved possible to extend the train to serve Darlington and Newcastle, which the namely blithely ignored, because it was still advertised as the *WEST RIDING PULLMAN*. The timings adopted in May were retained, but the portion servicing Harrogate now started from Newcastle at 9.10 a.m., left Darlington at 9.59 a.m, made a 10.34 a.m. call at Ripon before leaving Harrogate as before at 11.00 a.m. The Down train's Harrogate portion still arrived there at 8.49 p.m. but went forward to reach Darlington at 9.37 p.m. and Newcastle at 10.25 p.m. It did not call at Ripon and any passengers for that city were required to change into a local train which left Harrogate at 9.24 p.m. and after a 9.43 p.m. call at Ripon, that train went on to Northallerton, Eaglescliffe, Stockton and West Hartlepool.

Engines working this Pullman provided an interesting variety. Between Leeds and London both ways were a top link duty for King's Cross shed and their C1 class ex GN Atlantics really distinguished themselves on the $175^{3}/_{4}$ miles non-stop from and back to, Wakefield. In the years 1927 to 1932 they had strong competition from D11 ex GC 'Director' class engines of which three were then allocated to Copley Hill, for working London expresses. No.5511 went there in February 1927 but left in April 1928 when replaced by No.5501. In June 1931 that one was replaced by No.5510 until February 1933. Next to arrive was No.5507 which stayed from April 1927 to May 1932 although No.5502 substituted for it October 1930 to March 1931 as it had also done for No.5506 in January to May 1930 whilst Nos.5507 and 5506 went for general repair. No.5510 was also at Leeds from 29th November 1928 to 27th February 1929 whilst No.5506 had its previous general repair, that engine (now still active at

On a number of occasions Gorton shed sent a GC engine in substitution and here a D10 class is about to leave King's Cross termini with the *MANCHESTER PULLMAN*. Support for the train failed to reach a viable level so Manchester and also Sheffield lost Pullman service because this train ceased to run again after Saturday 19th September 1925.

Starting Monday 21st September 1925, two six-car Pullman trains were introduced between King's Cross and Leeds, running non-stop and worked by Top Shed C1's including the only one with four cylinders No.3279 seen here on the Up train south of Grantham early in 1928. The train was not named until 1st January 1927 when it then became the *WEST RIDING PULLMAN.*

Loughborough) having been one of the regulars at Leeds because it was shedded there from July 1927 until August 1932.

No.5503 also worked from Leeds but was only there from 25th July to 11th August 1928, clearly just to deal with extra traffic arising from the annual holiday period. By February 1933 all the D11 class had departed leaving the C1's in sole charge of the *WEST RIDING PULLMAN* non-stops. Between Wakefield and Bradford the motive power used was either a J1 or a J2 class 0-6-0 tender engine, and an 0-6-2 tank worked the Bradford-Halifax section.

Completely different classes were to be seen between Leeds and Newcastle, ex NER Atlantics of C7 class predominating, with occasional use of D49 and even A1 class Pacifics. In fact, on the last day for the Leeds-Newcastle section, No.2210 had the Up train and No.2574 took the final Down working. Most of that section was outside the West Riding of Yorkshire and combined with the NE Area's distaste for carrying headboards only once has it been found

that this train's engine ever carried one north of Leeds after their introduction in 1932. In contrast, they were carried regularly on the Leeds C1 class to and from King's Cross.

There was one exceptional and noteworthy instance of haulage on the non-stop running. On Thursday 15th May 1930, the Down train had special permission from the Chief Civil Engineer to be hauled through to Leeds by a Pacific and No.4474 of King's Cross shed was used. That was due to the train having two extra cars, taking the train weight to over 400 tons, to cater for an important French delegation who were travelling to London next morning. The weight restriction over the Calder river bridge, just south of Wakefield, then normally barred Pacifics from the Doncaster-Leeds line, so after No.4474 had traversed the bridge very slowly, the time lost was more than made up on the main line and the train reached London $1^{1}/_{2}$ minutes early.

The *WEST RIDING PULLMAN* traffic amply recompensed for the disappointing initial effort to

serve Nottingham, Sheffield and Manchester but the train so named ran for the last time on Saturday 28th September 1935. From the following Monday, Darlington and Newcastle had the advantage of the even better service from *THE SILVER JUBILEE* streamliner, so the Pullman was cut back to Harrogate. In lieu, for the first time, Hull was given Pullman service and also a $3^{1}/_{2}$ hour timing to and from London. That enabled a change of name from *WEST RIDING PULLMAN* to *YORKSHIRE PULLMAN.*

*(above)* The train name stemmed from it serving Leeds, Bradford, Harrogate, Halifax and Wakefield but until 1932 it was only carried by roof boards on the cars. No.3288 has the Up train at Doncaster on 10th September 1929.

*(left)* Until February 1927, King's Cross C1 class monopolised the working, one of them being No.4450, here backing out of King's Cross station after it had brought in the Up train non-stop from Wakefield.

*(opposite)* During 1927 three D11 class engines were sent to Leeds Copley Hill shed for working the *WEST RIDING PULLMAN* to and from King's Cross. No.5507 was there 1st April 1927 until 9th May 1932 and here has the Down train at Holloway in March 1928 whilst it was still in green livery.

*(opposite, top)* No.5506 was at Copley Hill from 2nd July 1927 until 29th August 1932 and here in 1928 on the Up train is coasting down into King's Cross.

*(opposite, bottom)* When No.5506 returned to Copley Hill on 27th February 1929, from a general repair, it had been repainted black, but still with its number on the tender. Here in 1930 it is near Hatfield on the *WEST RIDING PULLMAN*.

*(right)* D11 No.5502 had two spells at Copley Hill. Its first from 23rd January to 9th May 1930 allowed No.5501, and then No.5507 to be sent to Gorton for general repair. During that visit it was seen here on the Pullman at Marshmoor.

*(below)* No.5502 was again shedded at Copley Hill from 14th October 1930 to 6th March 1931, to allow No.5506 to go for general repair. Here, with its number moved to the cab, 5502 is on the Down train picking up water from Langley troughs. By 8th February 1933 all six D11 class which had worked from Copley Hill were returned to the GC Section.

*(left)* During the period when the D11 class were on the Pullman workings sometime in 1930, C1 class No.4419 of King's Cross deputised for one of them. On the Down train, here it is at Grantham.

*(below, left)* Starting 9th July 1928 the *WEST RIDING PULLMAN* was extended beyond Harrogate to Darlington and Newcastle, but any consequent change to the name was ignored. Workings between Leeds and Newcastle were done mainly by C7 class from Heaton shed. No.2197 in May 1930 has the Up train south of Darlington.

*(below)* In the 1934 summer Heaton used D49/2 No.293 as here on the Up train at Eryholme. It was the only D49 fitted with a speed indicator, which probably led to its being put on to this working. Note that no headboard was put on.

*(above)* A headboard for the engine was introduced in the 1932 summer and normally was always to be seen on the trains between Leeds and London. That year they reverted to haulage by C1 Atlantics allocated to King's Cross shed as here in 1933 on the Up train at Langley.

*(right)* This is the Down train at Potters Bar on 8th June 1935. Note the different letter spacing of 'West Riding' on the headboard.

*(opposite, top)* The *WEST RIDING PULLMAN* from Newcastle, Darlington and Harrogate passes Headingley station on 4th May 1934, hauled by C7 No.2200 of Heaton shed.

*(opposite, bottom)* Leaving Darlington, Heaton's C7 No.2196 is taking the *WEST RIDING PULLMAN* to Leeds (Central). North of Harrogate, was not the West Riding but only once from the introduction of headboards in 1932 to September 1935, when this train ceased running, was an engine headboard seen carried north of Leeds.

*(right)* The Up train here with No.4458 in charge is near Huntingdon. The *WEST RIDING PULLMAN* ran its last trips on Saturday 28th September 1935 because *THE SILVER JUBILEE* then made it redundant for Newcastle and Darlington passengers.

*(below)* From 30th September 1935 what had been the *WEST RIDING PULLMAN* had its name changed to *YORKSHIRE PULLMAN*. It continued to serve Harrogate and Leeds, Halifax and Bradford. Those two portions joining and splitting at Wakefield maintaining their service. A call at Doncaster was inserted as a portion for Hull was now provided. The complete train had a mile-a-minute booking both ways between King's Cross and Doncaster and in 1936 at Potters Bar A3 No.2751 has the Down train.

## YORKSHIRE PULLMAN

This name was used from Monday 30th September 1935, and apart from the hiatus due to the 1939-1945 war, survived for some years after steam locomotives ceased to haul it. Timings from Harrogate, Halifax, Bradford, Leeds and Wakefield were all made twenty minutes earlier, but the time taken by the Doncaster stop to attach the Hull cars was offset entirely by running the next 156 miles at a mile a minute, so London arrival time was also twenty minutes earlier at 2.40 p.m. The return train still left King's Cross at 4.45 p.m. and its sprint to Doncaster enabled West Riding arrival times to be retained. The Hull cars left that city at 11.10 a.m. and arrived back at 8.15 p.m. That scheduling was then kept for exactly two years, when the introduction of a streamlined express to serve Leeds and Bradford caused yet another alteration.

Introduced on 27th September 1937, the mid-morning departure of the *WEST RIDING LIMITED* from Leeds made their Pullman superfluous, so instead of the Harrogate cars going to Leeds, they were diverted via York to Doncaster where the four cars were joined by the two from Hull, and the two from Halifax, which now ceased to call and reverse at Bradford. The departure from Harrogate became 11.15 a.m., that from York 11.45 a.m. and from Hull at 11.30 a.m., for arrival in London at 3.00 p.m. The modernised D20 class No.2020 was transferred from York to Starbeck shed to cope with the Harrogate-Doncaster working. The London return departure was still kept at 4.45 p.m.

No engine headboard was provided until the changed arrangement started on 27th September 1937, and then it was in a single line of Gill sans showing *YORKSHIRE PULLMAN*. The engine from Harrogate usually brought the headboard into Doncaster, but there were many occasions in 1938 and 1939 of non-use between there and London. Nor was a headboard usually carried by the Hull portion

on the Doncaster shedded C1 which customarily worked it from Hull, although when it was once so carried, we are fortunate to have photographic evidence. From Doncaster to Hull a Botanic Gardens shedded D49 was normally used and was never seen carrying a headboard.

The fast runs south of Doncaster needed Pacific haulage and Classes A1, A3 and A4 from that shed were all used. Then, when new, V2 class became available, experience proved their 6in. smaller coupled wheels were no handicap on a mile-a-minute schedule, so they were also used. The normal complement was eight cars, but at weekends, that was frequently increased to as many as twelve. Even on weekdays it was essential to have prior seat reservation to be able to travel on the 4.45 p.m. from King's Cross. From July 1938 to the end of August 1939, the 4.45 p.m. provided frequent opportunities to travel at up to 90 m.p.h. behind the holder of the world speed record No.4468 MALLARD, because pre-war its home shed was Doncaster.

After the war-time withdrawal, a praiseworthy attempt was made to resume running of this Pullman, because it was substantially a businessmen's service. On 4th November 1946, A3 class HUMORIST, now No.97 instead of 2751, but restored to green livery, worked the first Up train and the Down one had No.107 ROYAL LANCER, both hauling nine cars. Despite its name, No.97 took the job so seriously that after its initial run, it did the next fifty-seven trips without a break. This flourish proved premature because in February 1947 this Pullman had to be withdrawn, due to the crisis in fuel supplies, coupled with abnormally severe winter weather and it was 6th October 1947 before its running could be restarted.

For the 1946 opening run a new deeper headboard was used, and had *THE YORKSHIRE PULLMAN* set in two lines. The pre-war single line board (without *THE*) was, however, brought into use again. By September 1948, both these painted boards

had been displaced by the first example of the cast plate which had beaded edge and raised lettering with a polished face. This showed just *YORKSHIRE PULLMAN* in two lines and was still being used into the 1960's.

Post-war there were only two portions, the main train leaving Harrogate at 10.15 a.m. and Leeds at 11.00 a.m. to which the Hull cars were attached at Doncaster and which left at 11.55 a.m. to be due into King's Cross at 2.50 p.m. Return had been advanced to 3.50 p.m. to arrive in Hull at 8.09 p.m. and Harrogate at 8.22 p.m. York had lost its Pullman service and there was no longer a Bradford and Halifax portion but there was still a call at Wakefield and the Hull cars also called at Goole. That is how the LNER handed it over to British Railways.

From September 1948, London departure returned to 4.45 p.m. and then in September 1949 it became 5.30 p.m. From 25th September 1950 it regularly had eleven cars, four of them in the Hull portion and two in a restored Bradford portion. Arrivals were 9.16 p.m. at Leeds, 9.42 p.m. at Bradford, 9.30 p.m. at Hull and 9.56 p.m. at Harrogate. The Up train left Harrogate at 10.07 a.m., Leeds at 10.45 a.m. and Hull at 10.30 a.m. to arrive in King's Cross at 2.38 p.m. In 1952, some ten minutes were cut from each run, the departure times remaining the same and that is how it substantially continued to the end of regular haulage by steam locomotives in 1961/2. Steam had been banned from King's Cross termini in June 1963 but this did not stop steam locomotives deputising for failed diesels on at least one occasion in 1963 and twice in April of the following year when 60114 and then 60054 did the honours.

*(opposite)* Both trains south of Doncaster now needed Pacific power, but the 2.40 p.m. arrival and 4.45 p.m. departure from King's Cross enabled an A3 or A1 shedded at Doncaster to work both the Up and Down trains. Here on 1st May 1937 A3 No.2747 is passing Sandy on the Down train.

*(left)* From 3rd March to 1st July 1938 Doncaster shed had three new A4's allocated to it and they lost no time putting them on to their Pullman working. Only four weeks old, No.4903 has the Down train at Potters Bar on 30th July 1938, and no headboard had yet appeared.

*(below)* Doncaster shed's No.4468 here has the Down train at New Southgate and on 4th August 1938 I saw their other A4 of the trio, No.4900 bring that train into Doncaster station.

*(right)* When a headboard did appear, later in 1938, it was the long, shallow type with lettering in Gills sans, light capitals. Pacific engines did not work this Pullman north of Doncaster station.

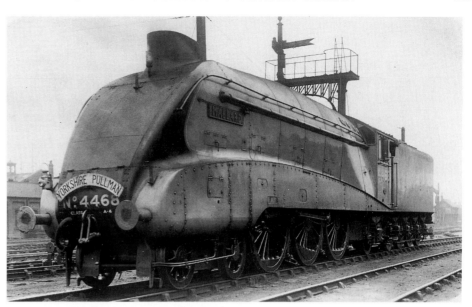

*(below)* The Hull portion of two Pullman cars was usually worked to Doncaster by a Doncaster shedded C1 class returning home, as No.3277 is doing here east of Hessle. The 6-wheel brake van would be detached at Doncaster.

*(left)* Even after the headboard was available, it was most unusual for it to be seen on the engine of the Hull portion, but that did occur at least once, No.4456 here arriving at Doncaster so fitted. Note the ordinary compartment carriage which the engine would take off with it at Doncaster.

*(below)* K3 No.231 moved to Copley Hill on 3rd August 1936 and here at Wakefield has the four cars which started at Harrogate and which it took over in Leeds (Central). After attachment of the cars from Halifax and Bradford, the K3 would work the combined train as far as Doncaster.

*(right)* The Halifax and Bradford portion was normally of two cars, and an N2 from Bowling shed worked it from Halifax into Bradford (Exchange) station were reversal was needed. No.2587 has that job here.

*(below)* N2 No.2590, here passing Ovenden at Easter 1937, is working three cars from Halifax to Bradford to cater for the extra traffic at that holiday.

*(below, right)* From Bradford, the Halifax cars were taken on to Wakefield to join those from Harrogate and Leeds, usually by one of the J1 of J2 mixed traffic 0-6-0's of Bowling shed. J2 No.3080 is arriving at Wakefield with them.

The introduction of the streamlined *WEST RIDING LIMITED*, on 27th September 1937, made the *YORKSHIRE PULLMAN* service from Bradford and Leeds redundant. So the cars from Harrogate to Doncaster were diverted via York to give that city a Pullman service as here in July 1938. The Halifax portion ceased its call and reversal in Bradford. It went direct to Wakefield and on to Doncaster. In contrast to previous custom in the NE Area, their Starbeck engine regularly carried the headboard.

*(above)* On one occasion in early 1939 the Harrogate portion had six cars instead of the normal four, so the regular Starbeck engine (the rebuilt D20 No.2020) was given assistance by their No.1217, a normal D20. Here the pair are working to Doncaster.

*(above, right)* Appreciable shuffling had to be done at Doncaster. Here A1 No.4470, the engine to go on to King's Cross, has taken over the four cars from Harrogate and will need to collect the two worked-in six minutes earlier from Hull, also the two from Halifax. In the Up direction the latter ran empty from Halifax, that town getting a connection at Bradford into the *WEST RIDING LIMITED* but retaining its Pullman service *from* King's Cross.

*(right)* The minimum load was four cars for Harrogate and two each for Halifax and Hull, but it often had to be augmented and on many weekends it was twelve cars. A1 No.4471 here has nine cars on the Down service at Brookmans Park in 1938.

Doncaster shed soon realised that the V2 class could do this fast and heavy duty with ease and their No.4817, new in February 1939, did a number of trips that year. On the Down train, here it is at Hadley Wood. Outbreak of war caused journey of the *YORKSHIRE PULLMAN* to be suspended after those run on Saturday 2nd September 1939.

On Monday 4th November 1946, a modified resumption of the *YORKSHIRE PULLMAN* was possible. The Harrogate portion reverted to running via Leeds and reversal in Central station, and here Starbeck's D49 No.2762 in December 1946 is arriving at Leeds from Harrogate. Although the pre-war headboard was carried, it looked incongruous when mounted on a D49 top lamp iron.

*(above)* This spring 1948 view of the Up train shows it about to enter Stoke tunnel south of Grantham and No.104 of King's Cross shed has the pre-war single line headboard showing only *YORKSHIRE PULLMAN*.

*(opposite, top)* A3 No.97 of King's Cross shed has the first Up train when the service restarted on 4th November 1946, and the normal load was nine cars. There were only two portions, the Harrogate cars served Leeds and Wakefield; those from Hull catered for Goole and Doncaster from where it was non-stop to and from King's Cross. A new headboard showed the name in two as *THE YORKSHIRE PULLMAN* in Gill sans type. The train is at Barkston.

*(opposite)* This train had to cease running in February 1947 due to the fuel crisis and the severe snowstorms being experienced throughout the country, but resumed on 6th October 1947. Here, at Potters Bar on 26th February 1948, King's Cross A3 No.107 has the Up train with ten cars and a bogie brake van. Note it is not carrying any of the three available headboards.

A3 class No.56 of King's Cross shed has the Up train approaching Potters Bar in April 1948, and carries a two-line post-war headboard. That one had thicker letters not as regularly spaced as the one done in Gill sans which can be seen in the view of 60047 on page 134.

*(right)* The Up nine car train on Saturday 11th October 1947, passing Brookmans Park, has Thompson B1 No.1112 of King's Cross shed. It had (appropriately) taken over at Hitchin from the A1/1 No.113 which had a hot box failure.

*(below)* The Thompson rebuilt Pacific which became No.113 did manage to work the Pullman successfully as here on the Up train south of the station at Potters Bar.

(left) On Thursday 27th May 1948, at Potters Bar, A3 No.60047 of King's Cross shed has ten cars on the Up train. This headboard is the post-war production with neatly spaced Gill sans lettering.

(below) By 25th September 1948, this cast headboard was in use and was adopted as the standard type thereafter. A2 No.60533 of King's Cross has the Up *YORKSHIRE PULLMAN* approaching Potters Bar. For this train's headboard there was reversion to two words, which in British Railways days was unusual.

(opposite) From the 1950 summer the Up train was worked by a Leeds Copley Hill engine instead of one from King's Cross. From June 1950 Copley Hill had nine Peppercorn Class A1's so almost invariably one worked the Up train, as No.60120 is doing here at Langley troughs.

King's Cross shed continued to work the Down train through the 1950's usually with an A3 or an A4. No.60003 here has it at Potters Bar with an eleven car load. On 29th August 1950, I was on the train when A3 No.60067's connecting rod broke exactly halfway at 70 m.p.h. near Holme and we were exceedingly fortunate not to be derailed at that speed.

A3 No.60067 LADAS in May 1961, has the Down train and is passing through Peterborough. This is the King's Cross based engine which nearly caused a disaster in August 1950. Here, No.60067 wears the newly fitted trough type smoke deflectors, and a new coat of paint, having recently visited Doncaster for its last 'General'.

29-8-50

# The Yorkshire Pullman escapes at 70 m.p.h.

THE Yorkshire Pullman narrowly escaped serious accident last night when a connecting rod —which joins the piston to the wheels —broke, south of Peterborough. The engine jolted its way along three-quarters of a mile of track before it could be pulled up. When the rod broke it was travelling at 70 miles an hour.

So thankful were the passengers for the courage of the driver and fireman that they took a collection for them, and shook them by the hand before they left Leeds Central Station. The train came in 100 minutes late.

The two men who saved the train are Joseph Howard (58), the driver, of Queen's Park, London, and James Howard (31), the fireman, of Hampden Crescent, London.

To the admiring passengers they soon became Joe and Jim.

*(right)* A3 No.60039 of King's Cross has the Down train at Knebworth on 24th June 1961 and still carries the headboard to which no plaques were applied. Note that the second to seventh cars are of those built in 1960 which did not have absolutely flat sides like the others built previously, of which the leading car is an example.

*(below)* In British Railways years the Hull portion as usually of four cars and here in 1960, passing Hessle, is going to Doncaster behind D49/2 No.62765. Occasionally a V1 or V3 2-6-2 tank would be used, No.67638 being seen to do so. These cars are all of 1928 built stock and post-war the engine on the Hull portion was never noted as fitted with a headboard, nor in a high state of cleanliness.

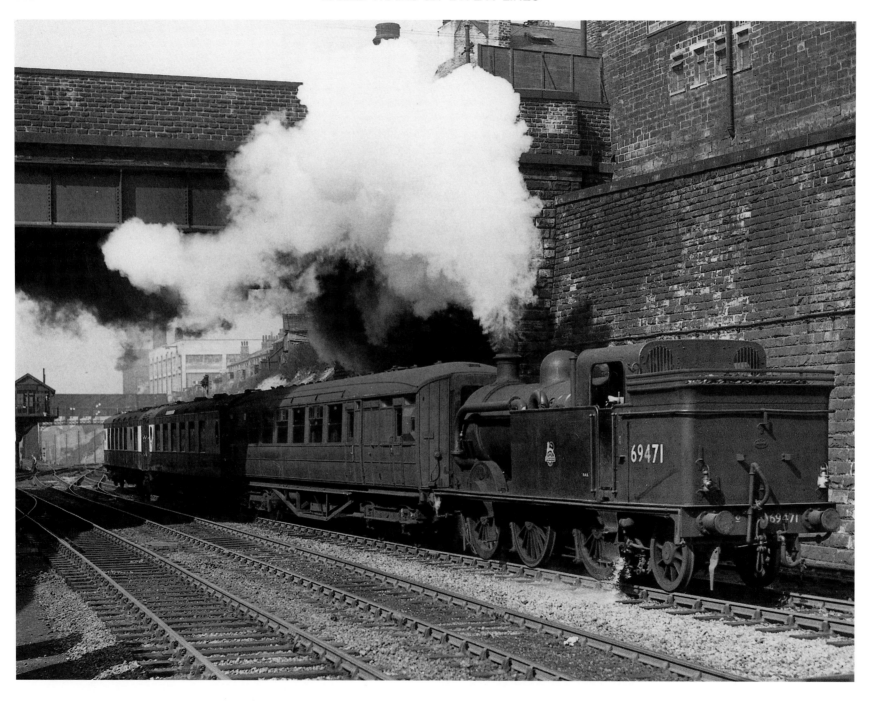

*(opposite)* The two cars comprising the Bradford portion also ran without a headboard when the Pullman service to and from Bradford (Exchange) was provided, starting again on 25th September 1950.

*(right)* A3 No.60069 left Gateshead for Leeds Copley Hill shed on 12th June 1960 and here at Walton, south of Wakefield, it has the Up *YORKSHIRE PULLMAN*. Use of an A3 (a filthy one at that) and the absence of a headboard rather indicates it was a late substitution for the rostered Copley Hill A1.

*(below)* The main Harrogate portion carried no headboard north of Leeds.

*(below, right)* New England shed's A2/2 No.60506 on the Up *YORKSHIRE PULLMAN* on 4th March 1961 at Hatfield was almost certainly in replacement of a Copley Hill engine which failed somewhere near Peterborough. 60506 was withdrawn on 4th April 1961 only a month after this trip.

A1 No.60120 was often on the Up train, and is here passing Leeds Copley Hill engine shed at the start of its southbound journey in the mid 1950's.

A1 No.60118 of Copley Hill here has the Up train at Beeston junction with the 1960 built cars. Diesel locomotives took over from steam power on a regular basis in 1962 but A1's and sometimes A3's deputised for failures. On 4th April 1964 A1 No.60114 took the train from Doncaster to King's Cross even though steam locomotives were officially banned from the terminus and less than a week later an A3, No.60054, by then a New England engine and only two months away from condemnation, did the honours.

Although it began to run in July 1927 and was named *HARROGATE SUNDAY PULLMAN* from May 1928, not until 1932 was a headboard introduced. Then it was as seen here, without inclusion of 'Sunday'. Until October 1936 King's Cross and then Copley Hill sheds worked it with C1 class between London and Leeds. Then A1's Nos.2553 and 2555 ran it until the war. No.2553 on the Down train is at Ardsley on Sunday 12th March 1939.

# WEEKEND PULLMAN & HARROGATE SUNDAY PULLMAN

Announced as a new *WEEKEND PULLMAN*, its first run was on Saturday 16th July 1927 at 4.50 p.m. from King's Cross to arrive Leeds (Central) at 8.15 p.m. and at Harrogate at 8.50 p.m. Return was at 3.15 p.m. from Harrogate, 3.50 p.m. from Leeds, on Sunday 17th to arrive in London at 7.15 p.m. It then ran each weekend until the beginning of May 1928.

This weekend arrangement did not prove sufficiently attractive, and was then changed. Advertised as the *HARROGATE SUNDAY PULLMAN*, that train started on Sunday 6th May 1928 at 10.30 a.m. from King's Cross to reach Leeds (Central) at 1.55 p.m. and Harrogate at 2.30 p.m. Quick servicing enabled the train to return from Harrogate at 3.15 p.m., Leeds at 3.50 p.m. and arrive in London at 7.15 p.m. Neither engine nor cars carried any indication of the train's name, and the headboard introduced in 1932, showed just *HARROGATE PULLMAN* in black on two lines on a white background. By 1939 the journey times were the same four hours overall, but the departure times were 10.00 a.m. from King's Cross and 3.00 p.m. from Harrogate.

Until the weight restriction on the bridge over the River Calder at Wakefield ceased in 1936, haulage between London and Leeds was by Class C1 Atlantics, but there could be more interesting

variety in what was used on the Leeds-Harrogate section, which was worked by engines shedded at Leeds Neville Hill. Normally, a D20 class 4-4-0 appeared, but on occasion a 4-6-2 tank of A8 class was used for that eighteen miles.

From the end of October 1936 it was possible to allocate Gresley Pacifics to Copley Hill shed at Leeds and until 1939, it was usual to see either No.2553 or 2555 on this Sunday train. When either was away for repair, Doncaster shed sent one of their A1 class in lieu.

The war caused the suspension of this service and when it was resumed again from Sunday 11th

June 1950, it took thirteen minutes longer for the Down journey, and twenty minutes more to London, due to the addition of a Bradford portion which needed extra time in Leeds (Central). Peppercorn A1 class now took a share in London-Leeds workings, but as late as August 1961, a 1923-built Pacific GAY CRUSADER was in charge. The post-war headboard carried *THE HARROGATE SUNDAY PULLMAN* set in three lines in white on a black background, supplanted in September 1950 by a cast plate with a beaded edge and raised letters and bright face. It was also good to see that plate carried through to Harrogate.

*(right)* Between Leeds (Central) and Harrogate, both trains were worked by North Eastern Area with an engine shedded at Neville Hill. Here, early in 1934, they used No.2147, which was newly rebuilt from Class H1 to A8 but, it was more usual for a D20 or D49 to work this job.

After the war, this train resumed on Sunday 11th June 1950 and had a 2-car Bradford portion added. A new headboard showed off the full name and at first was a black painted plate with white lettering. The usual engine was one of Copley Hill's Peppercorn A1's, No.60133 being at that shed's coaling stage.

(opposite) Copley Hill's A1 No.60134 is on the Up train between Rossington and Bawtry. A new cast headboard had replaced the painted plate and was one to which circular plaques were added, showing the arms of London and of Harrogate. It was in use by 13th July 1952.

It was rare for a North Eastern Region based engine to carry a headboard, its awkward position showing why. Here in early 1953, Starbeck's D49 No.62740 is leaving Harrogate for Leeds (Central).

*(opposite)* The Down train leaving King's Cross in August 1961 with the headboard still in use although the plaques had come off some years previously. Note A3 No.60108 was King's Cross allocated.

*(left)* For the 1923 summer, on Sundays only, a Pullman train made a return trip from London (Liverpool Street) to Clacton. Referred to as the *CLACTON PULLMAN*, the cars carried no identification. Here, on 24th June 1923, and still in GER painting, D15/1 class No.1848 is passing Stratford on its way to Clacton with a five car train.

*(below)* This Clacton train proved so popular that it soon needed seven cars and sometimes even eight, as D15/1 No.8828 has here going to Clacton on 15th June 1924.

# THE CLACTON PULLMAN  &  EASTERN BELLE

From November 1920, the Great Eastern Railway had included Pullman cars (both 1st and 3rds) in four main line trains in addition to the Hook boat trains. Those four trains served Cromer, Hunstanton, Lowestoft and Harwich (Town) from and to London (Liverpool Street). When the London & North Eastern Railway took over in 1923, all except the First Class cars in the boat trains were withdrawn, and as a consequence, an all-Pullman train could be assembled. On the summer Sundays of 1923, this was used to give Londoners a day at Clacton to skim off traffic which otherwise went to either Southend or Brighton.

Out of London at 10.00 a.m., the Pullman reached Clacton at 11.37 a.m. and departed Clacton at 5.10 p.m. and was into Liverpool Street at 6.45 p.m. Fares were £1 for First and 12/6d for Third Class and ordinary and season tickets could be used for 2/6d and 1/9d each way, subject to Pullman tickets being booked prior to joining the train. Refreshments and meals were also available.

No identification was carried in 1923, but a 1924 LNER advertisement did show it as *THE CLACTON PULLMAN*. Some (including Cecil J. Allen) referred to it as the 'Clacton Belle,' but no official recognition was ever given to that particular title. It continued to run in the summer Sundays of

1924 to 1927 but for the 1928 season, its official name became *THE CLACTON SUNDAY PULLMAN*, even though no such car roof boards were carried.

For the 1929 summer, more profitable use of the cars began by running them also on Mondays to Fridays for "half-day" trips, although London departures were between 11.00 and 11.50 a.m. Beginning on 3rd June 1929, the train usually went to Felixstowe on Mondays, to Clacton again on Tuesdays, to Frinton and Walton on Wednesday, to Dovercourt and Harwich on Thursdays and to Thorpeness and Aldeburgh on Fridays. Saturdays were given over to crew rest days and to train maintenance. From its 1929 start, it was officially titled *EASTERN BELLE*, and car roof boards were carried, but an engine headboard was only carried from 1933. In 1930 Skegness was substituted for a Harwich trip; that proved so popular that its inclusion was increased. The year also saw extension of longer journeys to such as Cromer, Hunstanton, Lowestoft and Yarmouth. Timings were frequently better than those for normal service trains, and it continued to run as the *EASTERN BELLE* until 1st September 1939. Then it became a war victim, because it never resumed.

By the 1927 summer the more powerful D16/1 class was the usual engine and No.8783 here is climbing Brentwood Bank with *THE CLACTON PULLMAN*.

For the 1928 summer its official name became the *CLACTON SUNDAY PULLMAN* but still without any such indication on the train. The time in Clacton was 5$^1/_2$ hours and here, leaving that resort, D16/1 No.8786 has one of the 1928 trains.

From the 1932 summer, an engine headboard was carried in addition to the car roof boards. On 19th July 1933 this train was going to Hunstanton and is at Shepreth junction behind Cambridge shed's Class D15/2 No.8882.

In 1933 the Down train is passing Brentwood station on its way to Yarmouth and has that shed's B12/1 No.8510 on the seven cars.

(opposite, far left) From 1929 summer the set of cars was also used from Mondays to Fridays to other seaside resorts. Here, on Wednesday 26th June 1929 at Frinton, D16/2 No.8787 is returning to London on the 7.55 p.m. departure from Walton. From June that year these trains had the official name of EASTERN BELLE and car roof boards showing that name were carried as here on seven cars.

(opposite, left) In 1930 longer trips were made by the EASTERN BELLE, and here nearing the GE station at that town it is approaching Cromer with a Norwich shedded Class B12/1 No.8570 in charge. For the 1938 season, Norwich shed turned out their newly acquired B17 No.2835 for the longish haul to Cromer.

(right) On Tuesday 29th May 1933, the usual seven car train is also going to Yarmouth behind that shed's D16/2 No.8800 and is passing Chadwell Heath.

*(above)* On Sunday 15th June 1930, the customary Clacton destination was taken by Stratford shed's B12/1 No.8552, the seven cars carrying *EASTERN BELLE* roof boards.

*(left)* In 1933 this *EASTERN BELLE* was strengthened to eight cars, and near Brentwood was being taken to Clacton by Colchester shed's newly rebuilt B12/3 No.8580.

The original 1932 headboard was not in Gill sans, but was repainted to that style by July 1933.

A selection of British Railways headboards at Grantham shed 21st October 1956, all in daily use and some looking the worse for wear. All these and other named trains will be fully covered in Part II.